Table of Contents

The Sacred and the Profane

Navigating the Catholic Influence on the Russian Literary Canon

by

Dr. ant

Although the author and publisher have made every effort to ensure that the information in this book was correct at press time, the author and publisher do not assume and hereby disclaim any liability to any party for any loss, damage, or disruption caused by errors or omissions, whether such errors or omissions result from negligence, accident, or any other cause.

This publication is designed to provide accurate and authoritative information with regard to the subject matter covered. It is sold with the understanding that the publisher is not engaged in rendering professional services. If legal advice or other expert assistance is required, the services of a competent professional should be sought.

The fact that an organization or website is referred to in this work as a citation and/or a potential source of further information does not mean that the author or the publisher endorses the information the organization or website may provide or recommendations it may make.

Please remember that Internet websites listed in this work may have changed or disappeared between when this work was written and when it is read.

The Sacred and the Profane: Navigating the Catholic Influence
on the Russian Literary Canon

Contents

<u>**Appendix B: A Comparative Analysis of the Original Russian Texts and Their Catholic Themes**</u>

Introduction: Catholicism and Russian Literature - A Sacred Union

The intricate tapestry of Russian literature is woven with threads of profound spiritual inquiry, ethical deliberation, and an unquenchable thirst for understanding the nature of the human condition within the divine order. At the heart of this cultural and literary exploration lies a subtle, yet potent, influence of Roman Catholicism—a tradition often viewed through the lens of its historical presence in Russia as both a religious and cultural other. This introduction embarks on a journey to elucidate the sacred union between Catholicism and classic Russian literature, with a specific focus on the works of Fyodor Dostoyevsky and Leo Tolstoy, whose writings vividly reflect the complex interplay of faith, morality, and existential quest that characterizes this relationship.

The impact of Catholic ideas and motifs on Russian literature is not immediately apparent to the casual observer, given the predominantly Orthodox Christian backdrop against which Russian culture and literature developed. However, a closer examination reveals that Catholic theology, philosophy, and imagery deeply influenced several Russian authors, infusing their narratives with a richness and depth that transcends denominational boundaries. This book aims to uncover these layers, demonstrating how Catholicism's universal questions of faith, suffering, redemption, love, and morality find poignant expression in the Russian literary canon.

Understanding this sacred union requires insight into the historical context and spiritual landscape of Russia, particularly during the times of Dostoyevsky and Tolstoy. These towering figures of Russian literature, each in their unique way, grappled with the existential dilemmas of their age, frequently dialoguing with Catholic theology—whether implicitly or explicitly—in their quest for truth. Dostoyevsky's exploration of free will, suffering, and redemption, alongside Tolstoy's search for God, ethical living, and rejection of dogmatic religion, provide fertile ground for examining the Catholic undercurrents in their works.

The symbiotic relationship between Catholic thought and Russian literary creativity is evident in the way these authors engage with themes central to Catholic theology—sin, forgiveness, the nature of divine justice versus human morality, and the quest for sanctity. Through their narrative and philosophical explorations, Dostoyevsky and Tolstoy embody the spiritual and ethical struggles that resonate deeply with Catholic doctrine, while also reflecting the universal human journey towards understanding one's place in the cosmos.

This book does not merely aim to catalog Catholic influences in Russian literature; rather, it seeks to offer a deeper understanding of how these religious ideas and themes are woven into the fabric of Russian narrative art, influencing its development and leaving a lasting legacy. By doing so, it also endeavors to exalt and propagate the core tenets of Catholicism—faith, hope, and charity—highlighting their enduring relevance and transformative power.

The journey through the chapters of this book will traverse diverse themes, from the role of saints and sinners to the presence of Catholic mysticism, contemplating the moral theology and eschatological visions present in Russian literature. Each theme will be explored with an eye towards uncovering the dialogue between Catholic thought and Russian literary genius, revealing the depths of a sacred union that has enriched both spheres.

Moreover, this exploration is intended to serve as a bridge, inviting readers from various backgrounds—Roman Catholics, Russian literature scholars, ethicists, moral theologians, and students—to engage with the rich tapestry of ideas and beliefs that unite Russian literature and Catholicism. It aims to foster a deeper appreciation of the universal questions that unite humanity in its search for meaning and transcendence.

Through a combination of expository, scientific, and philosophical writing styles, this book endeavors to articulate the intricate relationship between Catholicism and Russian literature in a manner that is both intellectually rigorous and accessible. By doing so, it hopes to contribute to a greater understanding and appreciation of the nuances and complexities that define this sacred union.

In conclusion, the union between Catholicism and Russian literature is not merely a matter of thematic overlap or philosophical curiosity. It represents a profound engagement with the deepest questions of human existence—questions that transcend cultural, linguistic, and denominational divides. As this book unfolds, it is hoped that readers will come to see Dostoyevsky, Tolstoy, and their contemporaries not just as literary giants, but as theological interlocutors who engaged with Catholic thought in ways that continue to enlighten, challenge, and inspire.

The Groundwork of Faith and Literature

In exploring the fertile void where theology meets artistry, it becomes apparent that the scaffolding of human experience is often erected from the materials provided by faith and imaginings. The intricate dance between the divine and the penned world has, across epochs, yielded narratives deeply imbued with spiritual questioning and revelation. Within the vast expanse of Russian literature, the tendrils of Catholic thought have woven themselves not only into the fabric of societal ethos but have profoundly influenced the literary canon, fundamentally shaping the works of luminaries such as Dostoyevsky and Tolstoy. Their texts, repositories of exploration and insight, serve as a testament to the indelible impact of Catholic doctrine on the reflective Russian soul (Givens, 2018).

At the heart of this intersection lies a rich historical tapestry, portraying a Russia wherein the Catholic faith, though not the majority creed, engaged in a silent dialogue with the nation's spiritual consciousness. This intersection facilitated a unique cultural synthesis, where the tenets of Catholicism seeped into literary expressions, thereby sculpting the philosophical contours of Russia's literary giants. The interplay between faith and literature in Russia is thus not merely a testament to religious influence on artistic expression but signifies a deeper, more intrinsic engagement with the questions of morality, existence, and the divine that occupy human contemplation. Within this framework, the definitive exegesis of Catholic influence is perhaps best articulated through the works of Dostoyevsky and Tolstoy, whose narratives are irrevocably intertwined with the existential inquiries and moral dilemmas central to Catholic theology (Harrison, 2013).

Therefore, to unravel the threads of Catholicism within Russian literature necessitates an examination not just of the historical presence of the faith in Russia, but of its manifestation within the literary canon as posited through the works of its most venerable writers. The codification of Catholic themes — sin, redemption, suffering, and divine grace — within their narratives not only underscores the universality of these concerns but also highlights the nuanced manner in which these authors grappled with them, thereby contributing to a broader understanding of human nature and divine providence. It is within this intricate tapestry of belief and narrative that the groundwork of faith and literature reveals itself, offering insight into the symbiotic relationship that nourishes both the soul and the story (Ramet, 1990).

Overview of Catholic Influence in Russia

The fabric of Russian literary tradition, deeply interwoven with the threads of spiritual and philosophical exploration, cannot be fully appreciated without acknowledging the subtle yet significant influence of Roman Catholicism. While the predominant narrative of Russia's religious landscape is characterized by its Orthodox heritage, the Catholic Church has played a pivotal role in shaping not just the spiritual but also the cultural contours of Russian society. This influence extends to the realm of literature, where the universal questions of faith, morality, and human existence are engaged with an intensity that mirrors the Catholic intellectual tradition.

In examining the Catholic influence on Russian literature, it is essential to recognize the historical context in which this interaction took place. The periods of religious schism, political conflict, and cultural exchange between the Western and Eastern Christian worlds have contributed to a unique spiritual synthesis within Russian literature. This synthesis manifests in the works of literary giants such as Dostoyevsky and Tolstoy, who, though not Catholic in the doctrinal sense, grappled with themes that are central to Catholic theology—such as redemption, free will, and the nature of evil. The depth with which these authors explore such themes can't help but evoke a dialogue with the Catholic intellectual tradition, even if indirectly (Givens, 2018).

Furthermore, the legacy of Catholic influence in Russia is not limited to thematic resonance alone but extends to the adoption of narrative strategies and philosophical inquiries that have their roots in the Catholic contemplative tradition. The introspective journeys of characters, their moral dilemmas, and the eventual illumination or redemption they experience, parallel the Catholic emphasis on personal conversion and the sacramental reality of grace in everyday life. This confluence of Catholic thought and Russian literature not only enriches the literary landscape but also offers a profound commentary on the universal human quest for meaning, morality, and transcendence beyond the mere material (Harrison, 2013).

The Historical Context and Spiritual Landscape This
exploration into the profound interplay between Catholicism
and Russian literature necessitates a dive into the historical
underpinnings and the spiritual terrain that defined Russia
during the epochs of Dostoyevsky and Tolstoy. The religious
landscape of Russia has been predominantly Orthodox Christian,
a faith that shares roots with Roman Catholicism yet diverges in
significant theological and liturgical aspects. This distinction set
a complex stage for the interaction between Russian culture, its
literature, and Catholic influences.

Throughout history, Russia experienced fluctuating degrees of
openness and resistance to Western religious influences,
including Catholicism. During the times of Dostoyevsky and
Tolstoy, the Russian Empire was in a state of spiritual and
ideological flux. The Orthodox Church held sway over the
spiritual life of the people, yet there was an undercurrent of
fascination and skepticism towards Western Christianity,
particularly Catholicism. This duality is reflected in the literary
works of the period, where one can discern a critical yet curious
engagement with Catholic themes and doctrines.

The 19th century, the era when Dostoyevsky and Tolstoy
penned their masterpieces, was marked by a quest for spiritual
and social renewal in Russia. The crumbling of feudal structures,
the rise of liberal ideas from the West, and the painful question

of serfdom formed the backdrop against which these literary giants worked. Their works, imbued with complex characters and profound ethical dilemmas, can't be fully understood without appreciating this quest for meaning in a rapidly changing world.

Within this historical context, the spiritual landscape was equally tumultuous. A noticeable divide existed between the formal, institutional practices of religion and the deeply personal, sometimes radical, spiritual quests of individuals. This dissonance is evident in the religious inquiries and themes prevalent in the works of both Dostoyevsky and Tolstoy. At times, their writings grappled with the essence of Christian morality, free will, and the problem of evil — themes that are central to Catholic theology as well.

The influence of Western European thought brought about by increased travel and the translation of foreign literature also introduced the Russian intelligentsia to Catholic philosophical traditions. Writers and thinkers were thus exposed to a wider array of religious philosophies, including those stemming from Catholicism, which challenged and enriched their understanding of their own Orthodox beliefs and practices.

In the works of Dostoyevsky, one encounters a profound engagement with the dilemmas of faith, suffering, redemption, and the nature of evil — themes that resonated deeply with Catholic theological discourse. For instance, his exploration of redemption through suffering in "Crime and Punishment" echoes the Catholic emphasis on penance and atonement.

Tolstoy, on the other hand, embarked on a quest for a universal Christian ethic that transcended denominational boundaries. His spiritual journey led him towards a radical interpretation of Christianity, emphasizing moral living and nonviolence. This quest, while critical of institutionalized religion, including Catholicism, nonetheless engages with the core of Christian ethical teachings which Catholicism deeply embodies.

The Russian spiritual and cultural context of the 19th century, thus, provided a fertile ground for Dostoyevsky and Tolstoy to explore and critique religious and moral themes. Their engagement with these themes was not limited to a purely Orthodox perspective but was enriched by their exposure to Catholic ideas, either through direct interaction or via the broader European intellectual milieu.

The reception of their works also reflects the complex relationship between Russian Orthodox believers and Catholic teachings. While the official Church and state often resisted Catholic influence, viewing it with suspicion, the laity and certain intellectuals were drawn to its moral rigor, its rich tradition of theological reflection, and its global perspective on Christian brotherhood and humanitarianism.

This historical and spiritual context underscores the nuanced relationship between Russian literature and Catholicism. The interplay between the two was not straightforward but rather a dynamic engagement, marked by curiosity, skepticism, and a shared quest for transcendent truth. This backdrop is crucial for understanding the depth of Catholic themes in the works of Dostoyevsky and Tolstoy and their lasting impact on Russian literature.

In conclusion, the historical context and spiritual landscape of 19th-century Russia set a complex stage for the interaction between its literature and Catholicism. Dostoyevsky and Tolstoy, each in his own way, grappled with the spiritual and ethical dilemmas of their time, engaging with Catholic themes amidst a predominantly Orthodox milieu. Their works reflect a Russia in search of its soul, standing at the crossroads of Eastern and Western Christian traditions. Through their literary exploration, they contributed to a broader understanding of Christian faith, morality, and human suffering, highlighting the universal quest for redemption and truth that transcends denominational boundaries.

Defining the Canon: Dostoyevsky and Tolstoy

In juxtaposing the literary journey of Fyodor Dostoyevsky and Leo Tolstoy with the theological and moral philosophies intrinsic to Roman Catholicism, a profound understanding of the symbiotic relationship between faith and literature emerges. Both authors, though operating within the largely Orthodox Christian framework of Russia, grappled with questions that are at the core of Catholic theology—free will, suffering, redemption, and the nature of divine justice. This exploration outlines how Dostoyevsky and Tolstoy, each in their unique narrative brilliance, engage with these themes, thus laying the groundwork for their unintentional yet invaluable contribution to the Catholic literary canon.

At the heart of Dostoyevsky's oeuvre is a profound interrogation of free will, a concept that Catholic theology holds with utmost reverence. His characters often find themselves at the crossroads of moral decision-making, embodying the Catholic view that human freedom is a gift, enabling love but also allowing for the possibility of turning away from God. Through works such as "The Brothers Karamazov," Dostoyevsky delves into the complexities of faith, doubt, and the possibility of redemption, exploring these ideas with a depth that resonates with the Catholic intellectual tradition.

Tolstoy, on the other hand, presents a quest for the essence of God and the true meaning of Christian life. Although he famously struggled with the institutional church, his spiritual journey and the characters he created reflect a constant search for the kingdom of God on earth, echoing the Catholic teaching that the divine permeates our daily lives. "War and Peace" and "Anna Karenina" demonstrate how understanding and compassion for the human condition lead to spiritual awakening—themes that align with Catholic emphasis on mercy and forgiveness.

The inclusion of Dostoyevsky and Tolstoy within a Catholic literary framework does not imply their adherence to Catholic doctrine but rather highlights their interrogation of existential dilemmas that align with Catholic thought. Their exploration of sin, redemption, the nature of evil, and divine grace speaks to universal questions that transcend denominational boundaries, thus earning them a place in the discussion of Catholic literature.

Dostoyevsky's narrative worlds are rife with suffering, a theme that occupies a central place in Catholic theology through the lens of the cross. Suffering, in Dostoyevsky's narratives, becomes a pathway to understanding, a means through which characters encounter their own limitations and their need for divine grace—a concept deeply embedded in Catholic teaching.

Tolstoy's ethical imperatives, particularly in his later works, emphasize love, nonviolence, and the moral responsibility of individuals to live a life in service of others. These principles reflect the Catholic call to charity—the love of God and neighbor—which stands as one of the highest virtues in the Catholic faith.

Both authors, through their complex characters and intricate plots, present a nuanced view of faith that challenges readers to reflect on their own beliefs and assumptions. This introspection, encouraged by Dostoyevsky's and Tolstoy's literary genius, mirrors the Catholic intellectual tradition, which values the use of reason alongside faith as a means to understand the divine and the human condition.

Furthermore, Dostoyevsky's and Tolstoy's works engage with the concept of personal conversion, a recurring theme in Catholic theology. Their characters often undergo profound transformations that illuminate the path from sin to redemption—a journey that illustrates the Catholic understanding of grace and forgiveness.

The dialogues on faith and reason found in the works of both authors also draw a parallel with Catholic tradition. The philosophical disputations in Dostoyevsky's novels and the introspective monologues in Tolstoy's works serve as literary arenas where faith and doubt, reason and revelation contest, and in doing so, reflect the Catholic emphasis on faith informed by reason.

In addition, both authors explore themes of death and the afterlife, engaging with concepts of judgment, heaven, and hell—central elements of Catholic eschatology. Their narratives ponder the meaning of human existence and destiny in the light of eternity, contributing to a deeper understanding of Catholic teachings on the afterlife.

This intertwining of theological themes with literary craftsmanship not only underscores the relevance of Dostoyevsky and Tolstoy to a Catholic literary canon but also showcases the universal appeal of their works. By exploring the existential questions that confront all of humanity, their literature transcends the boundaries of culture and creed, offering insights that are valuable to Roman Catholics, Russian literature scholars, moral theologians, and students alike.

Thus, the inclusion of Dostoyevsky's and Tolstoy's works within the study of Catholicism's impact on Russian literature does not assert a direct influence of Catholic doctrine on their writings. Instead, it acknowledges how their exploration of themes relevant to human existence and spirituality intersects with Catholic thought, enriching the Catholic literary tradition.

The respective literary contributions of Dostoyevsky and Tolstoy, when viewed through the lens of faith, are not just a reflection of their own spiritual quests but also a beacon for those who seek to understand the human condition in all its complexity. Their narratives, steeped in questions of faith, morality, and redemption, continue to engage readers in a profound dialogue on the essence of belief, the nature of sin, and the possibility of salvation.

In conclusion, Dostoyevsky and Tolstoy, through their indelible impact on literature and continual engagement with themes resonant with Catholic theology, are essential figures in defining the canon of Catholic literature. Their works, transcending the Orthodox Christian framework of their cultural and historical context, speak to the universal quest for meaning, morality, and redemption—a quest that is at the heart of the Catholic faith.

Catholic Theology in Dostoyevsky's Narrative

The exploration of Catholic theology within the rich tapestry of Dostoyevsky's literature unveils a nuanced dialogue between the profound depths of human suffering and the luminous promise of redemption. Dostoyevsky, though not a Catholic, interweaves Catholic theological concepts with a masterful precision, compelling his readers to confront their own existential dilemmas through the lens of faith. His narratives delve into the intricacies of free will, divine justice, and the transformative power of suffering, offering a profound commentary on the human condition that resonates with Catholic doctrinal teachings.

At the heart of Dostoyevsky's exploration lies the question of free will, a central tenet of Catholic theology. The depiction of characters who grapple with their capacity for good and evil serves not only as a reflection of the internal conflict inherent in every human soul but also echoes the Catholic understanding of free will as a gift, necessitating personal responsibility (Catechism of the Catholic Church, 1994). Through his characters' struggles, Dostoyevsky articulates the delicate balance between divine providence and human freedom, illustrating the complexities of navigating moral choices within the constraints of societal and divine laws.

The theme of suffering and redemption, another cornerstone of Catholic theology, permeates Dostoyevsky's works. Characters such as Raskolnikov in *Crime and Punishment* embody the profound turmoil of a soul in search of redemption through suffering. Dostoyevsky's portrayal of suffering as a crucible for spiritual purification closely aligns with the Catholic notion that suffering has redemptive value, offering a path to salvation and a deeper union with Christ in His Passion (John Paul II, 1984). This narrative alignment underscores a shared belief in the transformative potential of suffering when embraced with faith and repentance.

Moreover, Dostoyevsky's engagement with themes of divine justice versus human morality often mirrors Catholic ethical dilemmas. Through his intricate plots and morally ambiguous characters, Dostoyevsky challenges his readers to reflect on the nature of justice and mercy, both human and divine. His narratives wrestle with the tension between the temporal application of justice and the eternal perspective of divine mercy, inviting a contemplation of Catholic teachings on forgiveness, confession, and reconciliation. This theological inquiry not only enriches the moral complexity of his works but also fosters a deeper understanding of the mercy inherent in Catholic doctrine.

In conclusion, Dostoyevsky's narrative artistry offers a compelling exploration of Catholic theological themes, presenting a literary canvas where the struggles of faith, the paradox of free will, and the mystery of suffering unfold. While his works do not explicitly propagate Catholic doctrine, they profoundly engage with questions central to Catholic theology, making his narratives a fertile ground for dialogue between Catholic thought and Russian literature. In this interplay, Dostoyevsky's literary genius illuminates the depths of the human soul, echoing the Catholic quest for meaning in the midst of suffering and the relentless hope for redemption.

The Question of Free Will

The exploration of free will underpins significant narratives within Dostoyevsky's oeuvre, rendering an intricate examination of moral autonomy versed within the framework of Catholic theology. A pivotal aspect of his narrative scrutinizes how characters navigate their autonomy against the backdrop of divine grace and providence, presenting a complex interplay between human freedom and spiritual determinism. This tension elucidates a crucial theological discourse wherein the sacrosanctity of free will is affirmed, aligning with the Catholic doctrine which posits that free will is integral to human existence, allowing individuals to choose between good and evil (Catechism of the Catholic Church, 1993).

Dostoyevsky's protagonists are often depicted at the crossroads of significant moral decisions, embodying the Catholic understanding that while God's grace facilitates the choices leading toward salvation, it does not impinge upon the individual's freedom to choose. This dynamic is vividly portrayed through characters who wrestle with their inner demons, debating moral virtues against their temptations or despair. Such narratives are not merely literary constructs but resonate deeply with the Catholic viewpoint that free will is both a gift and a test, bestowed by a loving Creator who desires a genuine relationship with His creation predicated on love and not coercion (John Paul II, 1993).

Further, Dostoyevsky's exploration of free will extends into the realm of suffering and redemption, where characters often endure profound tribulations that challenge their spiritual beliefs and moral fortitudes. In this regard, the author masterfully illustrates Catholic theology's stance on redemptive suffering — the belief that suffering can be a means of sanctification and purification of the soul, ultimately leading one closer to God (Pope Benedict XVI, 2007). This concept underscores the transformative potential inherent in exercising free will, even amidst adversity, affirming the inherent dignity and value of human choice in the journey towards redemption.

Moreover, through his narrative, Dostoyevsky probes into the ramifications of misused free will, where characters' choices lead to sin and existential despair. This mirrors the Catholic teaching that while free will empowers individuals to pursue the good, it also confers the responsibility to bear the consequences of one's actions. The depiction of characters grappling with guilt and seeking redemption captures the essence of the Catholic sacrament of reconciliation, emphasizing the Church's role as a mediator in the restoration of the divine-human relationship compromised by sin (Vatican II, 1965).

In essence, Dostoyevsky's narrative serves as a profound commentary on the Catholic understanding of free will, encapsulating its significance in human existence and salvation history. Through the lens of his characters and their journeys, the narrative delves into the profundity of choice, the sanctity of moral struggle, and the hope of redemption, thereby offering a rich tapestry that both challenges and reaffirms the theological discourse on free will within the Catholic tradition.

Divine Justice vs. Human Morality The profound dialogue between divine justice and human morality reveals itself as a central theme not only in the theological realms but also within the intricate layers of classic Russian literature. This discourse, particularly visible through the lens of Roman Catholicism, manifests a complex interplay where divine laws intersect with the moral compass guiding human actions. The theological convictions of Catholicism, embracing both the rigorous demands of divine justice and the merciful nature of God's love, illuminate the literature of Dostoyevsky and Tolstoy in uniquely revelatory ways.

In Catholic theology, divine justice represents a fundamental attribute of God, encompassing both His judgment and mercy. It's a concept that transcends human understanding of justice, often confined to retributive or distributive modalities. This notion posits that divine justice, while encompassing the just recompense of deeds, is intrinsically linked to God's mercy, offering salvation and redemption to humanity. The paradox of a justice that simultaneously punishes and forgives underpins much of the moral conflict and narrative tension in Russian literature influenced by Catholic thought.

To juxtapose divine justice against human morality, one must consider the inherent fallibility and subjectivity of human moral judgments. Humans, in their limited capacity, often struggle with moral dilemmas where right and wrong are not easily discernible. The Catholic faith, however, introduces a dimension of absolute moral truths derived from divine revelation, thus framing human morality within a broader, transcendent context. This dichotomy between flawed human morality and infallible divine justice becomes a recurring motif in the works of Dostoyevsky and Tolstoy.

For instance, Dostoyevsky's exploration of free will confronts the existential responsibility accompanying human moral choices. Through his characters' struggles, he delves into the profound complexities of reconciling human actions with divine will. The tension arises from the Catholic perspective that while God's grace enables the exercise of free will, the choices made can align with or diverge from divine justice. It is within this space of moral ambiguity that Dostoyevsky illuminates the Catholic teaching on the necessity of redemption and the role of suffering.

Similarly, in Tolstoy's narratives, the search for moral significance in a seemingly indifferent universe questions the efficacy of human justice when compared to divine standards. Tolstoy's characters often embark on spiritual journeys motivated by a deep yearning for an absolute moral compass, reflective of their quest for divine justice in a morally relative world. Through these journeys, Tolstoy presents Catholicism's assertion that true moral fulfillment is found in aligning one's life with God's eternal laws, beyond mere human conventions.

The Catholic notion of confession and repentance as pathways to understanding divine justice further elucidates this thematic exploration in Russian literature. Both Dostoyevsky and Tolstoy employ these sacramental themes to highlight the transformative power of acknowledging one's sins before God. This sacramental act underscores the Catholic belief in God's infinite mercy, offering redemption to even the gravest sinner, thus presenting a divine justice that redeems rather than merely punishes.

In dissecting the interplay between divine justice and human morality, it's crucial to examine the Catholic perspective on the inherent dignity of every person. This doctrine posits that each individual is created in the image and likeness of God, thereby possessing an intrinsic value that surpasses all earthly judgments. This concept resonates within Russian literary works, where characters often confront societal injustices that diminish the value of the individual, advocating a return to the respect of divine image as the foundation of true justice.

The exploration of suffering and redemption within these literary narratives also speaks to the Catholic understanding of redemptive suffering. Suffering, when united with Christ's own, becomes a means of purification and sanctification, offering a pathway to divine justice through the transformative power of grace. This theological concept finds resonance in characters that endure suffering, not as an end in itself, but as a conduit to spiritual awakening and moral clarity.

Moreover, the Catholic eschatological vision of heaven and hell adds another dimension to the discourse on divine justice in Russian literature. This viewpoint underscores the ultimate realization of divine justice in the afterlife, where human souls are judged according to their deeds and intentions. The anticipation of this final judgment permeates the moral consciousness of characters, influencing their actions and decisions within the temporal realm.

Through these various thematic strands, Russian literature influenced by Catholicism offers a rich tapestry of reflections on the relationship between divine justice and human morality. By navigating the tensions between God's absolute moral law and human ethical dilemmas, these narratives provide profound insights into the complexities of moral living in a fallen world. They challenge readers to contemplate the nature of justice, both human and divine, and the possibility of reconciliation through redemption.

In conclusion, the interplay between divine justice and human morality, as explored in classic Russian literature through a Catholic lens, reveals the depth and breadth of the human condition in its quest for meaning and redemption. This thematic exploration not only enriches our understanding of literary narratives but also offers a reflective mirror on the moral and spiritual struggles inherent in human existence. As such, it invites a continued dialogue between faith and literature, between divine absolutes and human aspirations.

Suffering and Redemption

In exploring the profound relationship between Catholic theology and Fyodor Dostoyevsky's narrative, one cannot overlook the intricate themes of suffering and redemption that permeate his works. These motifs are not merely literary devices but are deeply ingrained in the theological underpinnings of Catholic doctrine, mirroring the path of Christ's Passion and Resurrection. Dostoyevsky's characters often undergo profound personal crises that lead them through a journey of suffering, eventually guiding them toward redemption.

The Catholic understanding of suffering is unique in its emphasis on redemptive suffering. This concept holds that human suffering, when united with the Passion of Christ, can become a source of salvation and purification, not only for the sufferer but for the world. In Dostoyevsky's narratives, this principle is vividly depicted through characters who experience profound spiritual awakenings after enduring great personal tribulations. Such transformations reveal Dostoyevsky's deep engagement with the notion of suffering as a cathartic and ultimately redemptive process.

Redemption in Dostoyevsky's works is often portrayed as a complex, multifaceted process, involving not just the resolution of individual guilt or sin, but a total transformation of the self towards the good. This mirrors the Catholic conception of redemption as an ongoing journey rather than a single act. Characters in Dostoyevsky's universe find redemption through love, forgiveness, and often, through a newfound relationship with the divine, echoing the Catholic belief in God's central role in personal transformation.

The character of Raskolnikov in "Crime and Punishment" serves as a poignant example of Dostoyevsky's exploration of suffering and redemption. His journey from crime, through suffering and alienation, towards eventual redemption, is emblematic of the Catholic understanding of penance and reconciliation. Raskolnikov's internal turmoil and external hardships ultimately lead him to a deeper understanding of humanity and compassion, underscoring the transformative power of suffering.

Similarly, the story of the brothers Karamazov reflects the complexity of human nature, sin, and the possibility of redemption through suffering and faith. Ivan's intellectual struggles with the existence of God and the problem of evil, Alyosha's spiritual purity and faith, and Dmitri's tumultuous path toward redemption encapsulate the Catholic assertion that suffering is an integral part of the human condition, with the potential to lead individuals closer to the divine.

Dostoyevsky's narrative also challenges and engages with the Catholic notion of 'felix culpa' or fortunate fall. This concept suggests that the Fall of Man, while tragic, allowed for the greatest good: Christ's Redemption. Through his characters' falls and subsequent journeys to redemption, Dostoyevsky explores the paradoxical idea that great spiritual heights are often achieved through suffering and sin, echoing the Catholic theology that out of sin can come greater good.

The role of free will in Dostoyevsky's portrayal of suffering and redemption is crucial. The author's characters often face moral dilemmas that require them to make choices leading either to further degradation or to redemption. This highlights the Catholic teaching that while God's grace is necessary for redemption, human beings must freely cooperate with that grace, reinforcing the agency of the individual in the process of their salvation.

In "The Idiot," Prince Myshkin embodies the Christ-like figure of pure innocence and unconditional love whose presence and suffering expose the moral vacuity and hypocrisy of the society around him. Myshkin's redemptive suffering brings about transformation in the lives of others, illustrating the Catholic belief in the redemptive value of innocent suffering and its potential to reflect Christ's salvific sacrifice.

The theme of confession plays a significant role in Dostoyevsky's treatment of suffering and redemption. The act of confession, deeply rooted in Catholic sacramental life, is depicted as a necessary step towards achieving forgiveness and reconciliation with God and humanity. Through confession, Dostoyevsky's characters often find the strength to confront their suffering and embark on the path toward redemption.

Furthermore, Dostoyevsky's exploration of theodicy – the vindication of divine goodness and providence in view of the existence of evil – through his characters' experiences and philosophical dialogues, connects deeply with the Catholic attempt to reconcile human suffering with God's omnibenevolence. This is especially evident in dialogues involving Ivan Karamazov, where the discussion touches on the essence of free will, suffering, and the possibility of redemption in a seemingly unjust world.

The influence of Dostoyevsky's Russian Orthodox background cannot be ignored in his treatment of these themes. However, his works reveal a profound and often critical engagement with Catholic theology, particularly in his exploration of suffering and redemption. This suggests that Dostoyevsky's exploration of these themes transcends denominational boundaries, speaking to universal human experiences and the search for meaning through suffering.

In conclusion, Dostoyevsky's narrative deeply resonates with Catholic theological principles, particularly in its portrayal of suffering and redemption. His characters' journeys through the depths of human despair to the heights of spiritual renewal not only reflect the Catholic understanding of the redemptive value of suffering but also engage with broader theological questions about free will, sin, and salvation. Through his exploration of these themes, Dostoyevsky offers profound insights into the human condition, making his works an invaluable resource for understanding the intricate relationship between Catholic theology and literature.

The Search for God in Tolstoy's Works

The endeavor to comprehend the divine has perennially coursed through the veins of human history, entwining itself with our literature and moral fabric. Leo Tolstoy's works, resplendent with questions of faith, ethics, and the nature of God, serve as a seminal case study in this grand quest. In exploring Tolstoy's spiritual journey, one witnesses an intricate dance with God, not as an entity to be merely worshipped within the confines of traditional religious structures, but as a profound, omnipresent force intimately linked to the ethical imperatives of love and nonviolence.

Central to Tolstoy's spiritual excavation is his seminal work, "The Kingdom of God Is Within You," embodying his radical reimagining of Christianity. Here, Tolstoy elucidates a Christianity stripped of churchly dogma and ecclesiastical pageantry, proposing instead a faith rooted in the realization of God's kingdom on Earth through adhering to Christ's moral teachings. His interpretation profoundly resonates with Catholicism's emphasis on the beatitudes as a path to encountering God, albeit diverging on ecclesiastical authority and ritualistic expressions of faith. This deviation underscores Tolstoy's belief in a personal, direct relationship with the divine, accessible through moral living and compassion (Givens, 2018).

Tolstoy's repudiation of violence and advocacy for nonviolence as a Christian imperative further cements his alignment with the ethos of 'turning the other cheek,' a principle echoing through Catholic teachings on peace and reconciliation. His letters and essays articulate a vision of society transformed through love and forgiveness, inviting a reflection on how these ideals are mirrored in the Gospels and resonated within the broader corpus of Christian ethical teachings. Yet, Tolstoy's pacifism, extending to a critique of state and church complicity in violence, challenges the institutional aspects of Catholicism, urging a return to what he perceives as the core of Christ's message (Harrison, 2013).

The ethical frameworks Tolstoy constructs invite a broader contemplation on the nature of divine love and the human capacity for moral discernment. His literary works, especially those grappling with moral dilemmas and the search for meaning, such as "War and Peace" and "Anna Karenina," reflect a profound engagement with the existential questions that also animate Catholic theology. Through the lens of his characters' struggles and epiphanies, Tolstoy probes the depths of human fallibility, grace, and redemption, themes that resonate with the Catholic sacramental understanding of confession and atonement (Green, 1986).

In sum, Tolstoy's exploration of God in his writings invites a dialogic engagement with Catholic thought, presenting both convergence and divergence on the nature of divinity, the role of the church, and the path to spiritual fulfillment. His works serve not only as a rich field for theological and ethical inquiry but also as a bridge for dialogue between different faith traditions, each seeking to answer the age-old question of how to live a moral life in communion with the divine.

The Kingdom of God Is Within You

In delving into the intricacies of Leo Tolstoy's spiritual journey, one cannot overlook his seminal work, "The Kingdom of God Is Within You," where he articulates a profound understanding of Christ's teachings, notably diverging from the orthodoxy of institutional religion. This section seeks to explore the intricate layers of Tolstoy's theology, particularly focusing on his interpretation of the Kingdom of God as an inner spiritual state rather than an external entity or a geographical realm. This perspective not only challenges traditional ecclesiastical structures but also aligns with broader Catholic contemplative traditions, which emphasize the immanence of God in the individual's soul.

Tolstoy's assertion that the essence of Christianity lies in the Sermon on the Mount and that the kingdom of God is to be found within each person, resonates with the Biblical passage, "The kingdom of God cometh not with observation: Neither shall they say, Lo here! or, lo there! for, behold, the kingdom of God is within you" (Luke 17:20-21, King James Version). This principle underscores an intimate, personal experience of the divine, which Tolstoy believed was obscured by the Church's emphasis on ritual and dogma.

By advocating for a direct and personal relationship with the divine, Tolstoy's views intersect with certain aspects of Catholic mysticism, despite his explicit rejection of organized religion. Catholic mystics throughout history, such as Teresa of Avila and John of the Cross, emphasized an intimate, experiential knowledge of God achieved through inner purification and contemplation. Similarly, Tolstoy's call for inner transformation through the practice of love, nonviolence, and poverty reflects Christ's beatitudes, highlighting a moral theology grounded in the transformation of the self rather than adherence to external religious practices.

Moreover, Tolstoy's interpretation of the Kingdom of God challenges readers to confront the ethical imperatives of their faith. He argues that Christianity's essence is not found in the observance of rituals or in submission to ecclesiastical authorities but in living a life of love, compassion, and nonresistance to evil. This radical interpretation of the Gospels invites a reevaluation of the role that institutional religion plays in guiding the moral and spiritual lives of believers.

At the heart of Tolstoy's theology is a vision of Christianity that transcends denominational boundaries, focusing instead on the transformative power of love as the ultimate expression of faith. His critique of the church's role in society - particularly its complicity with state power and violence - is a call to return to the foundational teachings of Jesus, which, according to Tolstoy, offer a blueprint for personal and social transformation.

This approach to Christianity, while controversial, opens up a critical dialogue with Catholic theology, particularly in the context of the Church's social teachings and its call to social action. Tolstoy's emphasis on the moral responsibility of individuals to live according to the teachings of Jesus resonates with Catholic calls for social justice, care for the poor, and peacemaking.

Thus, exploring "The Kingdom of God Is Within You" within the broader context of Tolstoy's works reveals a nuanced theological perspective that, despite its critical stance toward institutional religion, shares common ground with key aspects of Catholic thought and practice. It serves as a reminder of the rich, complex dialogue between faith and literature, and the enduring quest for understanding the divine in the midst of human experience.

In conclusion, Tolstoy's theological insights, as expressed in "The Kingdom of God Is Within You," not only challenge the reader to rethink the essence of the Christian faith but also offer a bridge between the mystical dimensions of Catholicism and the ethical imperatives of living a Christ-centered life. By focusing on the inner spiritual life of the believer and the call to embody the love and compassion of Christ, Tolstoy's work contributes to a broader understanding of the search for God in human life, transcending the boundaries of traditional religious institutions.

Tolstoy's Rejection of Dogmatic Religion The exploration into the depth of Leo Tolstoy's spiritual journey reveals a complex relationship with conventional religious practices and beliefs, particularly those delineated by the organized, dogmatic institutions of his time. Tolstoy's intellectual and spiritual quest led him toward a profound skepticism of established religious doctrines, which he viewed as not only inadequate but often contrary to the essence of Christian ethics as he understood them.

In the broader scope of Russian literature's dance with Catholicism, Tolstoy stands out not for the embrace but rather his deliberate distancing from the institutional side of Christianity. His writings, both fictional and philosophical, articulate this dissonance, pushing for a return to what he deemed the pure, undiluted teachings of Jesus Christ. This disjunction wasn't just a minor theme but a cornerstone of his later works and thought.

At the heart of Tolstoy's spiritual rebellion was his disillusionment with the Church's role in society. He saw a stark contrast between the Gospel's teachings on love, forgiveness, and poverty, and the Church's wealth, power, and punitive morality. This incongruity, he believed, undermined the Church's moral authority and distanced it from the true teachings of Christ. For Tolstoy, the church's alliance with state power was particularly troubling, viewing it as a betrayal of Christ's message of peace and love.

Tolstoy's journey toward this stark realization wasn't instantaneous but evolved through decades of contemplation, study, and reflection. In his pursuit of spiritual truth, he delved deeply into the Gospels, extracting what he saw as their essence and formulating a personal interpretation of Christianity that emphasized nonviolence, poverty, and love as its core principles.

This personal interpretation, however, led him to a critical standpoint regarding the necessity and validity of sacraments as practiced within the Orthodox Church and, by extension, other Christian denominations, including Catholicism. He questioned the efficacy and sincerity of ritualistic practices, suggesting that true faith and spirituality extend beyond the ceremonial into the realm of personal moral conduct and interpersonal relationships.

His seminal work, *The Kingdom of God Is Within You*, encapsulates Tolstoy's theological and ethical convictions. Here, he explicitly articulates his rejection of the church as an institution, advocating instead for a form of Christianity that is practiced through every action and interaction, free from the trappings of organized religion. This work, considered radical at the time of its publication, prompted significant backlash and further alienated Tolstoy from the Russian Orthodox Church.

Tolstoy's insistence on distinguishing between institutional religion and genuine spiritual life invites a critical examination of Catholicism's historical and theological development. While Tolstoy himself did not engage extensively with Catholic doctrine specifically, his critiques mirror concerns raised within Catholic circles regarding ritualism, clericalism, and the risks of spiritual complacency within structured religious life.

Despite his criticisms, Tolstoy's works offer invaluable insights into the essence of Christian ethics - insights that resonate with core Catholic teachings on love, mercy, and humility. His spiritual philosophy, emphasizing the transformative power of love and the importance of living in accordance with one's conscience, intersects significantly with Catholic social teaching and its emphasis on justice, peace, and the inherent dignity of the human person.

Understanding Tolstoy's rejection of dogmatic religion not only provides a window into his personal spiritual journey but also encourages a broader dialogue about the nature of faith, the role of religion in society, and the quest for authenticity in one's relationship with the divine. His critique invites believers and theologians alike to reflect on the essence of their faith and the ways in which institutional practices facilitate or hinder genuine spiritual growth.

In analyzing Tolstoy's spiritual narrative, it becomes evident that his rejection of dogmatic religion was not a rejection of faith itself but rather an impassioned plea for a return to what he perceived as the heart of Christian teaching. This distinction is crucial for understanding the complexity of Tolstoy's stance and its relevance to discussions about the role of organized religion in fostering genuine spirituality and moral integrity.

For scholars of Russian literature and theology, Tolstoy's perspectives offer a rich field for exploration. His writings challenge readers to consider the intersection of faith, morality, and social justice, and to re-evaluate the boundaries between personal conviction and communal religious life. His legacy, marked by a relentless quest for truth and a dedication to living according to his convictions, remains a compelling testament to the power of individual conscience over institutionalized dogma.

Ultimately, Tolstoy's spiritual odyssey underscores the perennial human search for meaning, morality, and connection with the divine. His rejection of dogmatic religion, with its insistence on personal integrity, ethical living, and the primacy of love, offers a provocative but deeply resonant perspective on the nature of true faith and the path toward spiritual fulfillment.

In conclusion, Tolstoy's life and writings embody a profound and challenging critique of organized religion, offering a perspective that, while controversial, invites ongoing reflection and dialogue on the essence and practice of faith. As such, his legacy continues to inspire those who seek to navigate the complex landscape of belief, ethics, and human spirituality in a quest for a more authentic and compassionate expressions of religious conviction.

The Ethical Imperatives of Love and Nonviolence

In the exploration of Tolstoy's pursuit of the divine, one cannot overlook the profound ethical imperatives of love and nonviolence that permeate his works. These principles, deeply rooted in the essence of Roman Catholic thought, serve as cornerstones for a transformative vision of human existence and social order. Tolstoy's ethical philosophy, much like the teachings of Catholicism, advocates for an unwavering commitment to love, compassion, and the renunciation of violence, drawing inspiration from the Sermon on the Mount and the example of Christ's life.

The notion of divine love holds a central place in Tolstoy's moral universe. This love is unconditional, universal, and self-sacrificing - characteristics that closely align with the Catholic understanding of agape. For Tolstoy, the practice of such love necessitates a radical reevaluation of societal norms and personal prejudices, urging individuals to extend compassion beyond the confines of familial and ethnic ties. This expansive love challenges the divisions wrought by nationality, social class, and religion, advocating for a fraternity that transcends worldly distinctions.

Integral to Tolstoy's ethical framework is the principle of nonviolence. Drawing from Catholic teachings on peace and the sanctity of life, Tolstoy condemns violence in all its forms - whether it be state-sanctioned warfare, capital punishment, or interpersonal conflict. He posits that violence only begets more violence, perpetuating a cycle of suffering that strays further from the path of spiritual and moral progress. Instead, Tolstoy champions the power of passive resistance and nonviolent action, strategies that later influenced eminent figures like Mahatma Gandhi in their quest for social justice and national independence.

These ethical imperatives are not mere abstractions in Tolstoy's oeuvre but are intricately woven into the fabric of his narratives. They manifest in the moral struggles of his characters, the societal critiques embedded within his plots, and the philosophical dialogues that punctuate his texts. Through these literary devices, Tolstoy invites readers to engage with profound questions regarding the nature of goodness, the efficacy of nonviolence, and the transformative potential of love.

The convergence of love and nonviolence in Tolstoy's ethical vision illuminates a path towards personal conversion and communal harmony. He advocates for a mode of living that mirrors the Beatitudes, urging individuals to embrace humility, meekness, and a hunger for righteousness. In doing so, Tolstoy articulates a version of Christian discipleship grounded in action, not merely belief, demanding an active commitment to the welfare of others and the pursuit of peace.

This ethical imperative extends to Tolstoy's critique of institutional religion and its complicity in perpetuating violence. He challenges the church's sanctioning of war and capital punishment, arguing that such endorsements are antithetical to the core teachings of Christ. Tolstoy's call for a Christianity that practices what it preaches reflects a longing for a church that truly embodies the ideals of love and nonviolence, resonating with the Catholic Church's modern efforts towards peacebuilding and social justice.

The synthesis of love and nonviolence in Tolstoy's thought suggests a radical reorientation of human society towards the ideals of the Kingdom of God. He envisions a world where individuals, guided by the principles of Christian ethics, eschew violence and embrace a universal brotherhood. This vision, deeply emblematic of Catholic social teaching, proposes a societal model characterized by equality, justice, and the inherent dignity of all individuals.

In conclusion, Tolstoy's ethical imperatives of love and nonviolence not only offer a profound critique of his contemporary socio-political context but also articulate a timeless vision for human flourishing. Inspired by the teachings of Christ and reflective of Catholic moral theology, these principles challenge individuals and societies alike to reimagine their relationships with one another and the divine. As we delve deeper into the search for God in Tolstoy's works, we find that his ethical philosophy, grounded in love and nonviolence, serves as a pivotal aspect of this spiritual quest, inviting us to participate in the construction of a more just and compassionate world.

The Prodigal Sons: Parallels in Narrative and Doctrine

Chapter 4 delves into the heart of both Catholic doctrine and Russian literary narrative, focusing on the motif of the prodigal sons—an allegory rife with themes of sin, confession, forgiveness, and, ultimately, redemption. The parallels between the doctrinal teachings of the Catholic Church and the narrative arcs crafted by the literary giants of Russia are not merely coincidental but are deeply embedded in the fabric of Russian storytelling, shaped by a profound engagement with spiritual themes. This exploration reveals how the parable of the Prodigal Son from the Gospel of Luke resonates with the spiritual and moral quests undertaken by characters in the works of Dostoyevsky and Tolstoy.

The concept of sin, which starts the journey of the prodigal son, is pivotal in understanding both Catholic doctrine and the development of characters in Russian literature. Sin, characterized by a deliberate turning away from the path of righteousness, sets the stage for a narrative of fall and redemption that is central to many Russian literary works. The Catholic Church's teachings on sin emphasize its nature as a betrayal of God's trust, requiring sincere confession and an intention to amend one's life (Catechism of the Catholic Church, 1994). Similarly, characters in Russian novels often face moments of moral crisis, leading to a recognition of their fallibility and an eventual reckoning with their sins.

Confession, both as a sacrament and a personal act of contrition, plays a crucial role in the journey back to righteousness. In Catholicism, confession is seen as a necessary step towards reconciliation with God, entailing an acknowledgment of sin, remorse, and the resolve to change one's ways. This mirrors the narrative arcs of characters who undergo a process of self-reckoning and disclosure, often portrayed through dramatic moments of dialogue or internal monologue, spotlighting the transformative power of articulating one's wrongdoings.

Forgiveness, the divine response to confession and repentance, is perhaps the most profound parallel between Catholic doctrine and Russian literature. The Church teaches that God's mercy is boundless, offering forgiveness to all who genuinely seek it (John Paul II, 1984). This theme of unconditional divine forgiveness is mirrored in the narratives, where characters who have acknowledged and repented their misdeeds are often granted a form of narrative redemption, experiencing relief from their moral dilemmas and a reintegration into the community or family—a clear nod to the prodigal son's return.

The return to faith, both in Catholic teaching and Russian storytelling, represents the culmination of the journey of the prodigal son. It signifies not just a return to religious belief but a profound interior conversion—a turning of one's heart towards goodness, truth, and love. This thematic element underscores the narrative arc of many protagonists in Russian literature, who, after enduring trials and tribulations that test their spirit, arrive at a deeper, more mature understanding of faith and their place in the cosmos.

The prodigal son motif, with its emphasis on moral fall and redemption, thus becomes a powerful narrative tool in Russian literature, reflecting a deep engagement with Catholic spiritual themes. The stories of Dostoyevsky and Tolstoy, imbued with questions of sin, suffering, and salvation, do not merely entertain but invite readers into a profound meditation on the nature of human freedom, the possibility of forgiveness, and the transformative power of faith.

It's imperative to discern that while the Catholic influence on Russian literature is unmistakable, it is not monolithic. The Russian cultural and philosophical milieu provided fertile ground for these themes to be explored in unique and varying ways. The adaptability and universality of the prodigal son narrative allowed it to be seamlessly woven into the fabric of Russian literary storytelling, transcending its doctrinal origins to speak to the universal human condition.

In conclusion, the journey of the prodigal son—as both a doctrinal allegory and a narrative motif—offers a rich vein of thematic material that has been masterfully mined by Russian authors. Their works reflect not only the moral and spiritual quandaries of their times but also the enduring human quest for redemption and the desire to return to a state of grace. Through their narratives, they engage with Catholic themes of sin, confession, forgiveness, and faith, illustrating the profound interconnection between literature and spirituality in the search for ultimate truth and reconciliation.

Sin, Confession, and Forgiveness

The intricate weave of sin, confession, and forgiveness forms a profound tapestry within the paradigms of Catholic doctrine and Russian literature alike. This symbiotic relationship, which underscores humanity's inherent fallibility and the Divine's mercy, is paramount in understanding the moral and spiritual undertakings of characters in the narratives of Dostoyevsky and Tolstoy. It is this interplay that provides the rich soil from which springs the exploration of redemption and human dignity.

At the heart of the Catholic faith lies the acknowledgment of sin as a fundamental human condition, a doctrine that finds a vibrant echo in the Russian literary landscape. The act of sinning, inherent to human nature, sets the stage for a journey towards redemption, a theme that both Dostoyevsky and Tolstoy intricately weave into the fabric of their characters' lives. The prodigal son, emblematic of this journey, not only embodies the fall from grace but, more importantly, the hopeful path toward reconciliation and renewal.

Confession stands as the sacramental gateway through which the sinner must pass to attain forgiveness. This act of humility and honesty before God is reflected in the candid introspection and subsequent confessions of characters, as they grapple with their internal turmoil and transgressions. It is within these moments of vulnerability that the narrative and the doctrine converge, illuminating the transformative power of admitting one's faults.

Forgiveness, in the Catholic understanding, is not merely an absolution of sin but a restoration of the individual to their original purity and a reaffirmation of their intrinsic worth. This divine mercy is mirrored in the literature's portrayal of characters who, despite their flaws and misdeeds, are capable of redemption. The message is clear: forgiveness is always within reach, a testament to the boundless capacity for change and growth.

Central to this discourse is the concept of free will, a pivotal element in the dynamic of sin and redemption. Both the Catholic Church and Russian authors champion the idea that humans, endowed with the liberty to choose, hold the keys to their destiny. This freedom, while allowing for the possibility of sin, also opens the door to redemption through conscious repentance and conversion.

In the narratives of Dostoyevsky and Tolstoy, sin is often portrayed not as an endpoint but as the beginning of a journey toward self-awareness and spiritual awakening. This mirrors the Church's teaching that sin, while to be avoided, can serve as a catalyst for deeper communion with God, should the sinner choose to turn back to Him. The prodigal son's return is emblematic of this belief, showcasing the power of contrition and the willingness to seek forgiveness.

Catholic doctrine emphasizes the communal aspect of confession and forgiveness, acknowledging that sin affects not only the individual but the whole community. Similarly, Russian literature frequently presents sin and redemption within a communal framework, reflecting on how individual actions resonate within the larger societal fabric. The stories of redemption are thus not isolated but interwoven with the lives of others, echoing the Church's view of humanity as fundamentally interconnected.

The sacrament of confession, with its emphasis on verbal acknowledgment of one's sins, underscores the power of words in the healing process. This sacrament's literary parallel can be seen in the pivotal confessional scenes that dot the landscapes of Russian classics, where the act of speaking one's faults becomes a cathartic pathway to liberation.

Forgiveness, within the Catholic perspective, is unconditional, a concept that challenges human notions of justice and retribution. This divine attribute of limitless mercy is reflected in the literary depiction of characters who, despite their transgressions, receive redemption. The narrative thus becomes a vessel for exploring the depths of forgiveness and the liberation it brings, both to the forgiver and the forgiven.

The journey from sin to forgiveness is often fraught with suffering and struggle, elements that both Catholicism and Russian literature do not shy away from. This suffering, however, is not pointless but serves as a purifying fire that burns away the dross of sin, preparing the soul for reconciliation with the Divine. The characters' trials and tribulations are thus imbued with a sense of purpose, highlighting the redemptive value of suffering.

Confession is also portrayed as an act of courage, a willing exposure of one's vulnerabilities and imperfections. This notion resonates with the Catholic understanding of reconciliation as a sacrament of healing. It is in the admission of weakness that strength is found, a paradoxical truth that unfolds within the pages of Russian classics as characters confront their darkest selves.

The ultimate promise of forgiveness, as presented in Catholic doctrine, is a restoration of relationship — with God, with oneself, and with the community. This holistic healing is mirrored in the narratives that celebrate reconciliation not just as a return to a state of grace but as a renewal of broken ties and the forging of new beginnings.

In conclusion, the dialogue between sin, confession, and forgiveness in Catholic doctrine and Russian literature reveals a shared belief in the human capacity for redemption and transformation. Through the lens of these narratives, we are invited to reflect on the profound truth that beneath the shadow of our failures lies the potential for grace, renewal, and a deeper communion with the Divine.

The Return to Faith

In considering the profound and intricate journey of the prodigal son back to faith, we must delve deeply into the human condition—a condition marked by a quest for meaning, a quest that both challenges and defines our spiritual and existential borders. It is within this quest that the narratives of classic Russian literature, particularly in the works of Dostoyevsky and Tolstoy, intertwine with Catholic doctrine in a dance that reveals much about the nature of belief, the pang of disbelief, and the powerful, often tumultuous, return to faith.

The notion of sin—integral to understanding the departure from and eventual return to faith—is portrayed with a complexity that respects the multifaceted nature of humanity. Sin is not merely an action violating divine law; it is a manifestation of the profound dissonance within the human soul, a departure from the natural order of things, and a disconnection from the Divine that Catholicism seeks to rectify. The narrative journey of a soul's return to faith, therefore, involves a reconciliation that is deeply personal and universally existential.

The Catholic understanding of confession plays a pivotal role in this reconciliatory process. The act of confessing not only signifies an acknowledgment of one's sins but also represents a profound act of humility and repentance—a desire to return to the state of grace. In its essence, confession is not primarily about seeking absolution from sin; it is about the restoration of a relationship, the rebuilding of a bridge between the soul and the Divine that sin has damaged.

Forgiveness, as viewed through the lens of Catholicism, is a divine attribute that the prodigal son seeks to experience on his return. It is a forgiveness that does not erase the past but transforms it, a forgiveness that is both a gift and a doorway to a new beginning. This concept mirrors the journey of many characters in Russian literature who seek redemption and find it not in the avoidance of their past but in confronting it, embracing it, and ultimately, transcending it.

The return to faith, therefore, is not a mere act of reintegration into a belief system. It is an existential homecoming, a return to one's essence and to a relationship with the Divine that had been obscured but never severed. It is a realization that, despite the detours and the distances traveled, the soul's ultimate destiny is to find its place within the divine order, to return to the source from which it sprung.

This journey back to faith is often marked by suffering, which, within the sphere of Catholic doctrine, holds a particular significance. Suffering is not seen as a divine punishment but as a path to transformation and purification. It is through the crucible of suffering that the soul is prepared for its return, stripped of illusions, and made ready to embrace the truth.

The narratives of Dostoyevsky and Tolstoy, replete with characters experiencing the darkest nights of the soul, reflect this understanding of suffering. These characters' returns to faith are not triumphant marches but weary, stumbling steps taken in the dark, guided by the faint but inextinguishable light of grace.

In their search for God, these characters embody the universal struggle with doubt, the temptation of despair, and the longing for certainty. Their journeys illuminate the Catholic teaching that faith is not a possession but a quest, not a static state but a dynamic movement toward the divine mystery.

The return to faith, as depicted in these narratives, is also a rediscovery of community. The prodigal son's journey is not just a return to the Father but a reintegration into the familial and communal fold. It underscores the Catholic vision of the Church not merely as an institution but as a spiritual family, a community of believers journeying together toward their ultimate home.

This communal dimension emphasizes the social nature of redemption. Salvation is not an isolated experience but a collective journey. The return to faith, then, involves a recognition of one's place within this spiritual family and a commitment to live out one's faith in the service of others.

The narratives of return in Russian literature, infused with Catholic doctrine, thus serve as a rich tapestry of the human search for meaning, a search that inevitably leads back to the core of one's being and the heart of the divine mystery. They remind us that the return to faith is a pilgrimage fraught with challenges but buoyed by hope, a journey inward that ultimately leads to an expansive embrace of the divine and the communal.

In synthesizing these insights, it becomes evident that the return to faith as depicted in the works of Dostoyevsky and Tolstoy, and as understood within Catholic teaching, offers a profound meditation on the human condition. It is a testament to the enduring power of grace, the possibility of redemption, and the inexhaustible capacity of the human heart for transformation.

Therefore, to journey with these prodigal sons through their narratives of sin, suffering, and redemption is to witness the unfolding of a deeply Catholic understanding of salvation history—a history in which every soul is called to a return, a reawakening to the beauty and truth of the faith.

In conclusion, "The Return to Faith" is not merely a narrative device but a spiritual reality mirrored in the lives of countless individuals who, guided by the light of Catholic doctrine and inspired by the rich tapestry of Russian literature, navigate their way back to the divine embrace. It is a journey that speaks to the heart of humanity's eternal quest for meaning, belonging, and ultimate fulfillment.

Chapter 5: Saints and Sinners - Character Archetypes

The exploration of character archetypes within the realm of classic Russian literature, particularly through the lens of Roman Catholicism, unveils a rich tapestry of saints and sinners. These character archetypes are not just mere constructs but are deeply rooted in the Catholic theological understanding of human nature, sin, and redemption. The quintessential figures of saints and sinners in the works of Dostoyevsky and Tolstoy embody the perennial struggle between virtue and vice, illuminating the profound moral and theological questions that pervade human existence.

At the heart of Catholic teaching is the belief in the inherent dignity of the human person, created in the image of God yet marked by original sin. This theological premise serves as a backdrop for the character development seen in Russian literature, where characters often embark on a tumultuous journey towards sanctity or perdition. Saints in these narratives often emerge not as paragons of perfection but as flawed individuals who undergo profound transformations through suffering, repentance, and grace, mirroring the Catholic understanding of sanctification (Catechism of the Catholic Church, 1994).

Similarly, the portrayal of sinners in Russian literature provides a nuanced exploration of the human condition. These characters, while often depicted as being ensnared in vice or moral ambiguity, are not beyond the reach of redemption. This reflects the Catholic concept of divine mercy and the possibility of conversion, reaffirming the belief that no one is so far gone that they cannot be brought back into the fold of God's grace. The dynamic interplay between grace and free will, central to Catholic theology, is vividly portrayed through the internal struggles and eventual outcomes of these sin-soaked characters.

The archetype of the sinner's journey towards sanctity is a recurring motif that resonates with the Catholic sacramental understanding of confession and reconciliation. Through this spiritual journey, characters not only confront their own weaknesses and failings but also experience the transformative power of forgiveness and redemption. This process echoes the Catholic emphasis on penance as a path to spiritual renewal and holiness (John Paul II, 1984).

In conclusion, the character archetypes of saints and sinners in Russian literature serve as a profound manifestation of the intricate interplay between Catholic theological concepts and human experience. By examining these archetypes, readers gain insights into the complexities of the human heart, the nature of sin, and the redemptive power of grace. Through the lens of

Catholicism, the narratives of Dostoyevsky and Tolstoy not only depict the moral landscapes of their characters but also invite readers to reflect on their own journey towards sanctity or perdition.

The Role of the Clergy and Monastic Life

In exploring the sinuous relationship between Roman Catholicism and Russian literature, particularly through the eyes of literary giants like Dostoyevsky and Tolstoy, one cannot overlook the pivotal role played by the clergy and monastic life. These figures and their chosen way of living encapsulate the essence of Catholic values, embodying the struggle towards sanctity while navigating the pervasive presence of sin in the human condition. They stand as intermediaries between the divine and the mundane, guiding characters and, by extension, the reader through the moral and spiritual labyrinths that define our existence.

The clergy, endowed with the responsibility of shepherding the flock, often find themselves entangled in the same web of sin and redemption that captures all humanity. Their portrayal in Russian literature serves not only as a critique of their moral and spiritual fortitude but also as a reflection of the community's aspirations and failings. Through their actions, both noble and ignoble, these clerical characters illuminate the complex interplay of divine grace and human free will.

Monastic life, with its emphasis on asceticism and contemplation, offers a stark contrast to the worldly pursuits that dominate much of human endeavor. Monks and nuns, in their ceaseless quest for closer communion with God, embody the ultimate rejection of temporal desires in favor of spiritual riches. Their existence, characterized by prayer, fasting, and labor, stands as a testament to the possibility of transcending the material to attain a glimpse of the divine.

Yet, it is through their flaws, their struggles, and occasionally, their falls from grace, that these clerical and monastic characters truly resonate with the audience. They underscore the message that sanctity is not the absence of sin but the persistence in seeking redemption, echoing the central tenets of Catholic doctrine. Their journeys, replete with temptations and trials, mirror the spiritual odyssey of every believer, offering both caution and hope.

Moreover, the inclusion of such figures and themes in literature serves a didactic purpose, imparting moral and theological lessons within the fabric of the narrative. They act as conduits through which complex Catholic doctrines are made accessible to the lay reader, fostering a deeper understanding of concepts such as confession, penance, and atonement.

In the monastic's renunciation of worldly ties and the clergy's engagement with the laity, one perceives the dual path of Catholic spirituality: the contemplative and the active. This duality underscores the Church's teaching that holiness can be pursued in various states of life, each with its unique challenges and means of grace.

The intersection of Catholicism and Russian literature, particularly through these archetypes, also serves to critique the institutional Church while celebrating the spiritual richness it offers. Through characters that range from saintly to deeply flawed, authors probe the human capacity for sanctity amidst adversity, highlighting the Church's role in fostering or, at times, hindering this quest.

The aesthetic portrayal of the clergy and monastic individuals in Russian literature does not merely entertain; it invites introspection. It beckons the reader to reflect on their spiritual journey, encouraging them to find parallels between their struggles and those of the characters. Through this reflective process, literature becomes more than a mirror to society; it transforms into a catalyst for personal conversion and growth.

This portrayal also contextualizes the broader socio-religious themes prevalent in the works of Dostoyevsky, Tolstoy, and their contemporaries. The clergy and monastics serve as symbols of the eternal struggle between good and evil, acting out the dramatic tension between the city of God and the city of man on the stage of literature.

In conclusion, the role of the clergy and monastic life in Russian literature is multifaceted, serving both as a mirror to societal values and as a beacon guiding the reader towards deeper spiritual understanding. Their depictions are instrumental in articulating the profound interplay between sin and sanctity, offering a rich tapestry through which the influence of Catholicism on Russian literary tradition is vividly illustrated.

The Sinner's Journey Towards Sanctity

The pathway from sin to sanctity is a thematic vein that runs deeply through the roots of Russian literature, intertwining notions of Catholicism with the complex fabric of human existence. This journey, emblematic of the penitent returning to the fold, is not merely a narrative device but a profound exploration of the soul's capacity for transformation.

Central to this exploration is the concept of free will, the bedrock upon which the edifice of moral and spiritual development is erected. The sinner, beset by the chains of his own making, stands at the crossroads of salvation and damnation, a testament to the Catholic understanding that grace is both a gift and a challenge.

The narrative testimonies embedded in the annals of Russian literature often portray this journey as arduous, fraught with internal and external battles. These stories do not shy away from the darkness that lurks within the human heart, nor do they deny the potential for redemption that lies dormant, awaiting a spark of divine grace.

Suffering, a theme as old as humanity itself, emerges as both a crucible and a teacher in this journey. It is through suffering that the sinner becomes acutely aware of his own frailties, drawing him closer to a recognition of his need for divine mercy. Here,

Catholic theology intersects with human experience, suggesting that suffering can be a doorway to deeper understanding and intimacy with God.

Confession, within this context, transcends the mere act of verbalizing one's sins. It becomes a sacrament of healing, a ritual of re-entrance into a state of grace. The act of confession, so vividly depicted in these literary works, is not only about the articulation of wrongdoing but about the transformation of the self.

Forgiveness, the pivotal moment in the sinner's journey, is portrayed not as a simple absolution of sins but as a complex, often painful process of reconciliation with God, the self, and the community. This reflects the Catholic understanding that forgiveness is both a divine gift and a human endeavor requiring humility, patience, and love.

The return to faith, then, is not a mere resumption of practices and beliefs but a profound reorientation of one's life and priorities. The sinner, now penitent, discovers in faith a wellspring of meaning and purpose that transcends his previous understanding.

Sanctity, the ultimate goal of this journey, is depicted not as a state of moral perfection but as a continual striving for holiness and communion with God. The saints, those who have trod this path before, serve as guides and intercessors, embodying the hope that even the most wayward can find their way home.

The role of the Church as a sanctuary and guide in this process is crucial. It offers not only the sacraments but also a community of support, a tangible manifestation of God's mercy and love. Through the Church, the penitent is reminded that his journey is not a solitary endeavor but a communal pilgrimage toward the divine.

Yet, this journey is not linear. It waxes and wanes, marked by moments of clarity and periods of desolation. Doubt and despair often cloud the path, challenging the penitent's resolve and faith. Yet, these moments too are part of the journey, for in the darkness, the light of grace can shine brightest.

The reintegration into the community, a crucial step in the journey, signifies not just the conclusion of a personal odyssey but the beginning of a new chapter in the life of the penitent and the community. It is a testament to the power of redemption and the possibility of renewal, as the sinner, now sanctified, takes his place once again among the faithful, bringing with him the lessons gleaned from his pilgrimage.

Ultimately, the journey from sin to sanctity is a mirror of the human condition, reflecting our innate longing for connection, meaning, and transcendence. It reminds us that no one is beyond redemption, that every soul has the potential for sanctity, and that the path to holiness is paved with grace, perseverance, and the transformative power of love.

In the final analysis, the sinner's journey towards sanctity serves as a powerful narrative of hope, underscoring the Catholic conviction that redemption is always possible, that grace abounds, and that the journey back to God—though fraught with challenge—is replete with the promise of peace and the fulfillment of our deepest longings.

Through their vivid portrayals of this journey, Russian literature not only provides a rich tapestry of human experience but also offers profound insights into the spiritual odyssey that lies at the heart of the Catholic faith.

This exploration of the sinner's journey towards sanctity, while deeply rooted in Catholic theology, transcends denominational boundaries, speaking to the universal human experience of sin, suffering, redemption, and the perpetual quest for meaning and connection.

Chapter 6: Catholic Symbols and Imagery

The nuanced tapestry of Catholic symbols and imagery weaves itself prominently throughout classic Russian literature, embodying both ethereal and earthly dimensions. At the heart of this exploration are the sacraments and sacramentals, elements filled with profound theological depth, yet presented in a manner that touches upon the human experience with a palpable intensity. These symbols serve not only as keystones of faith but also as literary motifs that enhance thematic coherence and character development.

Sacraments, in Catholic theology, are considered outward signs of inward grace, instituted by Christ. Literary interpretations of these sacraments in Russian texts often explore the complexities of faith, doubt, and redemption. Baptism, for instance, is frequently depicted as a metaphor for rebirth or transformation, resonating deeply with characters undergoing profound internal changes. Similarly, confession and penance are portrayed as pivotal moments of self-realization and reconciliation, both with oneself and the divine.

Sacramentals, though not sacraments per se, hold significant ritual and symbolic value within Catholicism. These include holy water, the rosary, or even the act of blessing oneself with the sign of the cross. In Russian literature, these elements often appear at critical junctures, serving as tangible reminders of the divine presence within the narrative. They help to blur the lines between the sacred and the profane, infusing ordinary moments with a sense of spiritual significance.

The cross, as a central symbol of Catholicism, epitomizes the paradoxical nature of suffering and salvation. This emblem of ultimate sacrifice and love is deeply embedded in the character arcs of many protagonists. Through their own crosses—be they physical, emotional, or spiritual—characters embark on journeys of suffering that ultimately lead to moments of grace and redemption. The cross transcends its physical form, becoming a symbol of the endurance and hope that characterize the human condition.

These symbols and imagery are not arbitrary but are meticulously chosen to reflect the inner workings of the characters' minds and the universe they inhabit. They serve as a bridge between the seen and the unseen, the tangible and the intangible, reminding both characters and readers of the inexorable connection between the divine and the mundane. The interplay of these symbols within the narrative fabric elevates the story to a realm where every gesture, object, and word becomes laden with multiple layers of meaning.

The application of Catholic symbols and imagery in literature also invites readers to reflect on their own spiritual journey. Through the lens of familiar sacraments and sacramentals, the narrative becomes a mirror, reflecting back not just a story but a profound spiritual examination. This reflection fosters a deeper engagement with the text, encouraging a contemplative reading that resonates on a personal level.

Moreover, these symbols often challenge characters and, by extension, readers, to confront their own beliefs, prejudices, and assumptions. They spark questions about the nature of suffering, the path to redemption, and the complexity of human free will. The literary exploration of these themes through Catholic symbols and imagery enriches the narrative, providing a multi-dimensional experience that transcends the bounds of ordinary storytelling.

In conclusion, Catholic symbols and imagery in Russian literature are not merely decorative elements but are deeply imbued with meaning. They enrich narratives with layers of spiritual significance, enhancing character development and thematic expression. As readers journey through these texts, they are invited to navigate the intricate landscape of faith, doubt, and redemption, guided by the luminous beacon of these sacred symbols.

Sacraments and Sacramentals as Literary Motifs

In the vast and profound ocean of classic Russian literature, one cannot overlook the currents of Catholic symbols and imagery, especially the use of sacraments and sacramentals as literary motifs. These elements, deeply embedded within the narrative structures and character arcs, serve not merely as theological constructs but as profound expressions of human experience and divine interaction.

The sacraments, embodying pivotal moments of grace and spiritual transformation, are intricately woven into the fabric of character development and plot progression. Baptism, for instance, is often depicted not just as a ceremonial initiation into faith but as a symbol of death and rebirth, echoing the tumultuous transformations characters undergo. This sacrament, serving both as an end and a beginning, provides a rich tapestry for exploring themes of identity, belonging, and redemption.

Confession, another sacrament richly utilized in literature, offers a dramatic arena for characters to confront their deepest sins, guilt, and moral dilemmas. Through the sacrament of Reconciliation, characters traverse a path from inner turmoil to peace, reflecting the broader narrative quest for truth and absolution. It's within these sacred confessions that the tension between divine justice and human frailty reveals itself, offering readers a mirror to their own complexities and aspirations for forgiveness.

The Eucharist, as the source and summit of Christian life, finds its way into literary narratives as a symbol of unity, sacrifice, and the profound mystery of divine love. Characters' participation in this sacrament, or at times their poignant absence from it, can signify moments of profound spiritual insight, community belonging, or profound isolation and longing.

Marriage, as a sacrament, is deployed to explore the themes of covenant, fidelity, and the sanctity of human love. Through the lens of marriage, literature examines the intertwining of human and divine love, the challenges of self-gift and sacrifice, and the quest for authentic relational unity that mirrors the divine.

Holy Orders and the Anointing of the Sick, though less frequently depicted, offer narratives a context to delve into themes of vocation, service, suffering, and the passage to eternal life. Through these sacraments, characters encounter the call to a life beyond themselves, a surrender to divine will, and the sanctification of their earthly journeys, even amidst pain and impending death.

Beyond the seven sacraments, sacramentals such as holy water, rosaries, or icons serve as tangible expressions of faith and channels of divine grace within literature. These objects, often interwoven into the daily lives of characters or pivotal plot moments, underscore the incarnation of spiritual realities in the material world.

Holy water, for instance, may be employed to signify cleansing, protection, or spiritual combat, echoing the sacramental theme of renewal and sanctification. Rosaries may appear as symbols of prayerful perseverance, Marian devotion, or the link between the temporal and eternal. Icons, imbued with profound religious significance, can serve as windows to the divine, focal points of spiritual quest, or manifestations of faith's tangible presence in the mundane.

Through these sacraments and sacramentals, literature illuminates the complex interplay between the human and divine, the physical and spiritual realms. They provide a lexicon of symbols through which the ineffable mysteries of faith, the drama of human redemption, and the quest for divine encounter are articulated.

Moreover, the integration of sacraments and sacramentals into narrative frameworks speaks to the sacramentality of existence itself, suggesting that all of creation is a potential medium of divine grace and revelation. In this sense, literature becomes a sacramental space, where the word becomes flesh in the characters and stories that resonate with the human condition's depth and transcendence.

In essence, the use of sacraments and sacramentals as literary motifs serves not merely to decorate but to deepen the narrative exploration of faith, identity, and redemption. These elements invite readers into a contemplative engagement with the narrative, beckoning them to see beyond the surface and encounter the sacred within the profane.

Thus, in classic Russian literature, sacraments and sacramentals are not mere artifacts of religious tradition but vibrant threads woven into the human story's fabric. They serve as bridges between the seen and unseen, the individual and the universal, the temporal and the eternal, illuminating the path toward understanding, reconciliation, and communion.

In conclusion, the exploration of sacraments and sacramentals as literary motifs opens up a multifaceted dialogue between faith and culture, literature and theology, unveiling the profound ways in which Catholic imagination infuses the narrative landscapes of classic Russian literature. Through this lens, readers are invited to reflect on their own spiritual journeys, inspired by the profound sacramental vision that underlies and elevates the human experience.

The Cross: Suffering and Salvation

In the fabric of Roman Catholicism, the Cross stands as the quintessential symbol of both suffering and salvation. This emblem, etched deeply into the doctrines and visual narratives of the faith, transcends its physical form to embody the profound theological significance of sacrifice, redemption, and unconditional love. The Cross's dual nature as both a symbol of torment and a beacon of hope offers an intricate lens through which one can explore the complex underpinnings of Catholic influence on Russian literature, particularly in the works of luminaries like Dostoyevsky and Tolstoy.

The paradox of the Cross, whereby agonizing death gives way to everlasting life, serves as a critical thematic pivot in Catholic teachings. It underscores a fundamental belief in the power of suffering as a pathway to transcendence and redemption. This notion, deeply woven into the narratives of both Dostoyevsky and Tolstoy, illustrates the indelible stamp of Catholic symbolism on the ethos of Russian literature. Through their characters and plots, these authors grapple with the existential realities of pain, sacrifice, and the quest for salvation, mirroring the theological essence encapsulated by the Cross.

At the heart of Catholic theology lies the Crucifixion – an event that epitomizes the ultimate act of love and self-sacrifice.

Christ's willingness to endure the Cross, to bear the weight of humanity's sins, and to offer Himself as a redemptive sacrifice illuminates the path to salvation through suffering. This narrative, fraught with agony yet radiant with hope, resonates powerfully within the dense, introspective layers of Russian literary masterpieces.

The Cross, therefore, is not merely a symbol within the Catholic tradition; it is an existential journey marked by suffering, sacrifice, and eventual redemption. Russian literature, with its profound examination of the human condition, naturally intersects with these themes, exploring the depths of despair and the luminous potential for redemption. The characters crafted by Dostoyevsky and Tolstoy often traverse dark valleys of suffering, their paths echoing the Via Dolorosa, yet within these narratives lies the profound potential for salvation, much like the resurrection that follows Christ's crucifixion.

In the realm of Catholic symbolism, the Cross functions as a tangible reminder of the vicissitudes of the human experience – embodying loss, despair, hope, and renewal. Similarly, in Russian literature, the Cross thematic serves as a potent metaphor for the spiritual and moral trials faced by individuals. These narratives delve into the complexities of faith, doubt, moral struggle, and the redemptive power of suffering, mirroring Catholic teachings on the salvific value of suffering endured in union with Christ.

Furthermore, the Cross in Catholicism is a representation of the intersection between the divine and the human, the temporal and the eternal. This convergence is vividly portrayed in Russian literature, where characters and narratives consistently straddle the temporal concerns of earthly existence and the eternal questions of faith and morality. The Cross symbolizes this intersectionality, offering a rich thematic vein that Russian authors exploit to explore the most profound questions of existence.

The embracing of the Cross, in Catholic teachings, signifies a willingness to accept and transcend suffering, embodying an act of faith in God's sovereign plan. This theological concept finds resonance in the literature of Dostoyevsky and Tolstoy, where characters often confront and ultimately embrace their suffering as a means of spiritual purification and redemption. Through this embrace, the narratives underscore the transformative power of suffering - a key tenet of Catholic theology regarding the Cross.

Moreover, the Cross's imagery in Catholicism is infused with the promise of resurrection and eternal life, offering a vision of hope and renewal beyond the pain of the present moment. This eschatological dimension enriches the thematic tapestry of Russian literary works, where the specter of death and the possibility of redemption through suffering are recurrent themes. The authors draw on this imagery to explore the dialectic between despair and hope, sin and salvation, underscoring the redemptive potential inherent in human suffering.

In sum, the Cross as a symbol of suffering and salvation deeply informs the thematic and existential landscapes of Russian literature. It serves as a bridge between the human and the divine, the individual and the universal, the temporal and the eternal. By embedding this symbol within their narrative structures and character arcs, Dostoyevsky and Tolstoy engage with the core tenets of Catholic theology, reflecting the profound interplay between faith, suffering, and redemption. Thus, the Cross not only embodies the essence of Catholic teachings but also illuminates the spiritual and existential quests at the heart of Russian literary tradition.

In conclusion, the Cross's enduring presence in Catholicism as a symbol of both crucifixion and resurrection offers a profound theological and philosophical framework within which Russian literature frequently operates. The interweaving of these themes - suffering as a path to redemption, the salvific power of love, and the promise of resurrection - showcases the intricate ways in which Catholic symbols and imagery enrich the narrative depth and spiritual complexity of Russian literary masterpieces. Through the prism of the Cross, readers are invited to explore the depths of human despair and the pinnacle of divine grace, tracing the arc of redemption that lies at the heart of both Catholic theology and Russian literary tradition.

Chapter 7: Dialogues on Faith: Philosophical Disputations and Inner Monologues

The intersection of faith and reason, particularly within the sphere of Catholicism, manifests profoundly in Russian literature, through both overt philosophical disputation and the nuanced introspection of inner monologues. This duality unveils the complexity of spiritual discourse, embodying a struggle that is at once deeply personal and universally human. Within these literary domains, iconic characters traverse the vast landscapes of belief, atheism, and the relentless quest for divine truth.

The intellectual struggle with atheism is not merely a plot device; rather, it serves as a critical reflection on the societal and existential doubts pervading the era. Characters grapple with the absence or presence of God in a world rife with suffering, querying whether faith can indeed coexist with the apparent randomness of pain and injustice. This tension mirrors the broader philosophical debates of the time, debates that questioned the very foundations of religious conviction and moral absolutes.

Simultaneously, discernment of divine will emerges as a compelling narrative force, pushing characters to confront their deepest fears and desires in the light of an unseen and, at times, unfathomable divine plan. The nuances of this discernment are laid bare in moments of solitude and despair, where the heart speaks louder than the mind, revealing an intimate dialogue between the self and the divine—a dialogue that, at its core, seeks understanding amid the turbulence of human existence.

These literary explorations are deeply emblematic of the Catholic intellectual tradition, which has long posited faith and reason as complements rather than adversaries. The synthesis of this viewpoint within Russian literature offers a rich tableau for examining how characters and, by extension, readers navigate the perennial quest for meaning in a seemingly indifferent universe.

Yet, this dialogue between faith and skepticism is not a stalemate. It is, instead, a dynamic journey that propels characters toward a deeper reckoning with life's ultimate questions. Through their trials and tribulations, characters often encounter a transcendental dimension of reality, one that silently affirms the presence of a greater purpose and the ineffable mystery of God's grace.

Moreover, this chapter illuminates the profound moral and ethical implications of these spiritual journeys. The quest for faith is invariably intertwined with the pursuit of virtue, as characters face the daunting challenge of aligning their actions with their burgeoning spiritual insights. This alignment is fraught with conflict and contradiction, yet it is precisely through this struggle that the potential for genuine transformation emerges.

Indeed, the dialogues on faith encapsulated in Russian literature resonate with the core tenets of Catholicism, which advocates for a faith that is both lived and experienced. It is a faith that does not shy away from doubt but embraces it as a pathway to deeper understanding and communion with the divine.

In conclusion, the philosophical disputations and inner monologues that permeate these literary works reflect a vibrant tapestry of faith, doubt, and renewal. They encapsulate the human condition in its rawest form, offering insights that are at once profoundly Catholic and universally human. Thus, through these narratives, literature becomes a sacred space where the soul's dialogue with faith and reason finds its most poignant expression.

The Intellectual Struggle with Atheism

The odyssey of faith is seldom a straightforward journey, particularly against the backdrop of an intellectually rich and tumultuous period. The confrontation with atheism, for the seekers of truth within the cloisters of Russian literature influenced by Roman Catholicism, represents not just a crisis of belief but a profound philosophical disputation. This struggle, emblematic of a broader existential inquiry, delineates a landscape where the mind and the soul find themselves in an intense dialectic. The depth of this interaction unveils the contours of atheism not as a mere negation of divinity but as a pivotal chapter in the individual's quest for meaning in the specter of an absent God.

At the heart of this intellectual struggle lies the perennial question: Can man's existential dread and the universe's seeming indifference reconcile with the concept of a benevolent Creator? This query, far from being a mere rhetorical exercise, plunges the faithful and skeptic alike into the abyss of doubt and despair. In this abyss, the foundation of one's belief system is relentlessly tested, and atheism emerges not solely as disbelief in God but as a critical evaluation of human existence in a seemingly godless universe.

The literature, suffused with Catholic motifs, buttresses this struggle, providing a canvas where characters grapple with the Divine's absence or silence. This exploration goes beyond theological debate, weaving into the narrative fabric of life's paradoxes and the human condition's complexities. These stories are not indictments but reflections, mirrors held up to a society navigating the chasm between faith and reason, between the visible and the invisible.

The intellectual struggle with atheism also manifests through the lens of moral theology. The quandary of moral good and evil underpins much of the discourse, raising poignant questions about divine justice and human autonomy. In a world rife with suffering and injustice, the specter of atheism challenges the believer to reconcile these realities with the notion of an omniscient, omnipotent, and benevolent deity. This tension, rather than obfuscating, can illuminate the profound depths of charity, forgiveness, and mercy as hallmarks of a lived faith.

Moreover, the Catholic intellectual tradition, with its emphasis on natural law and reason, offers a unique vantage point to engage with atheism. Rather than shunning the intellect, this tradition invites a dialogue where faith and reason are not adversaries but allies in the search for truth. This dialogic approach, reflective of the broader Catholic endeavor to integrate faith with human experience, underscores the belief that the seeds of faith can thrive even in the soil of doubt.

Furthermore, the sacramental imagination intrinsic to Catholicism enriches this struggle, endowing the material world with a transcendental significance. In the face of atheism, the sacramental worldview affirms the potential of the visible to convey the invisible, the mundane to manifest the divine. This sacramental perception, woven through literature, invites a re-enchantment of the world, a seeing beyond the surface to the divine mystery pervading all of creation.

The personal narratives of conversion, often depicting a return from the brink of nihilism, shed light on atheism as a stage in the spiritual journey rather than its terminus. These stories of transformation emphasize the role of grace, the moments of epiphany where the intellectual impasse yields to a deeper, ineffable understanding. Through these accounts, atheism is presented not merely as a philosophical stance but as a crucible through which the soul passes on its way to a more profound faith.

One might posit that atheism, in its essence, poses vital questions that faith must confront to remain vibrant and relevant. It compels a deeper engagement with the mysteries of existence, suffering, and the divine, challenging the believer to articulate a faith that resonates with the complexities of the human experience. In this light, atheism can be seen as a catalyst for a more mature, examined faith.

In conclusion, the intellectual struggle with atheism within the context of Catholic influenced Russian literature dazzles with its complexity and depth. It reveals a battleground where the soul wrestles with the shadow of doubt, emerging not weakened but fortified by the ordeal. The journey through atheism, fraught with challenges and epiphanies, exemplifies the dynamic interplay of faith and doubt, a testament to the human spirit's indomitable quest for meaning, belonging, and transcendence in an ambiguous universe.

Discerning Divine Will

In our exploration of the intricate relationship between Catholicism and Russian literature, a pivotal area of investigation emerges in the realm of theological discourse: the discernment of divine will. This complex subject bears significant weight in understanding the moral and ethical dimensions within the works of Russian literary giants. It is crucial, therefore, to delve into the philosophical underpinnings and theological debates that illuminate the struggle to interpret and embrace God's will in human life.

The discernment of divine will, as depicted in literature, often mirrors the inner turmoil and existential quests faced by characters. These literary portrayals encapsulate a profound engagement with faith that goes beyond mere doctrinal adherence, reflecting a personal and often tumultuous journey towards understanding and accepting God's plan. This struggle is not only a testament to the human condition but also serves as a bridge between the divine and the mundane, highlighting the interplay between free will and divine providence.

Within the Catholic tradition, discerning divine will is a multifaceted process that involves prayer, reflection, and often, the guidance of spiritual directors. This process is underscored by the belief that God communicates His desires to individuals, offering directions for a life that fulfills His purpose. However, the interpretation of these divine signs is subject to human frailty and limitations, resulting in a nuanced and sometimes contested understanding of what God truly desires from and for His creations.

The literary works of Dostoyevsky and Tolstoy provide fertile ground for examining these themes. Their characters frequently grapple with the notion of divine will, against the backdrop of moral dilemmas and spiritual crises. It is through these narratives that the authors navigate complex theological and philosophical terrains, challenging readers to reflect on the nature of God's guidance in their lives.

For instance, the concept of divine justice versus human morality, a recurrent theme in Dostoyevsky's oeuvre, prompts us to question the extent of divine intervention in the realm of human affairs. Dostoyevsky's characters often struggle with the reconciliation of God's will with the existence of evil and suffering, delving into the depths of human consciousness to unearth answers to age-old theological inquiries.

Similarly, Tolstoy's exploration of ethical imperatives, such as love and nonviolence, underscores his quest for understanding divine will in the context of human actions. His emphasis on the "kingdom of God is within you" reflects a personalistic approach to discerning divine will, where the inner spiritual transformation of the individual takes precedence over external ritualistic expressions of faith.

It is through this personalistic lens that both authors engage with the concept of divine will, challenging readers to consider the implications of their free will decisions in light of a divine plan. This dialectic between free will and divine will underscores much of the moral and spiritual tensions present in Russian literature, offering insights into the broader human quest for meaning and purpose.

Moreover, the role of suffering and redemption in understanding divine will is critical in the narratives of both authors. Suffering, as a vehicle for spiritual purification and redemption, often emerges as a divine mechanism for bringing characters closer to understanding God's will for them. This perspective aligns with Catholic teachings on redemptive suffering, wherein personal trials are viewed as opportunities for spiritual growth and closer alignment with divine intentions.

In addressing the discernment of divine will, it is crucial to consider the historical and cultural contexts that shaped the theological views of Dostoyevsky and Tolstoy. The Russian socio-political landscape, marked by upheaval and spiritual longing, provided a rich backdrop for the exploration of these themes. The intersection of Catholic theology and Russian orthodox traditions further complicates this landscape, offering a unique vantage point for examining how divine will is interpreted and manifested in literary narratives.

The challenge of discerning divine will, as portrayed in Russian literature, ultimately reflects the universal human experience of seeking guidance and purpose in a world that often appears indifferent or hostile to spiritual aspirations. Through their complex characters and intricate plots, Dostoyevsky and Tolstoy invite us into a deep engagement with the mysteries of faith, encouraging a reflective and nuanced approach to understanding God's plan for humanity.

As we conclude this discussion, it becomes evident that the journey towards discerning divine will is not a solitary endeavor but a collective one, shared by characters, authors, and readers alike. It is through this shared journey that we uncover the transformative power of literature to bridge the divine with the human, offering glimpses into the profound depths of spiritual inquiry and the quest for ultimate truth.

In drawing upon the rich tapestry of Catholicism and Russian literature, this section has endeavored to shed light on the pivotal role of discerning divine will in understanding the moral and spiritual dimensions of human existence. It is a theme that not only enriches our appreciation of literary masterpieces but also deepens our spiritual introspection and quest for meaning in the face of an ever-complex world.

The Virgin Mary in Russian Literature

The portrayal and invocation of the Virgin Mary in the vast expanse of Russian literature is a phenomenon that both perplexes and fascinates. As one delves into the marrow of Russian classics, it becomes evident how Theotokos, the Mother of God, emerges not only as a celestial intercessor but also as a profound symbol of maternal compassion, embodying the Church itself. The intricacies of these portrayals reveal a nuanced interplay between the doctrinal beliefs of Roman Catholicism and the spiritual landscape of Russia, a realm where Orthodoxy predominantly prevails.

Within the works of Russian literary giants, the Virgin Mary is often depicted with an aura of divine compassion and mercy, attributes that resonate deeply with Catholic Mariology. This echo of Catholic reverence toward Mary serves as a testament to the interwoven nature of Russian literature and Catholic spirituality, defying the ostensible religious boundaries. Such veneration is particularly palpable in the textual tapestry of Dostoyevsky, where Mary's intercessory power emerges as a lighthouse guiding the tormented souls towards redemption.

The symbolism of Mary as the Mother of the Church is multifaceted, reflecting her role as a nurturer and protector. In literature, she transcends her biblical origins, becoming a universal symbol of maternal love and sacrifice. This transformation is not incidental but a deliberate artistic choice that underscores the universal need for a compassionate intercessor in the face of life's tribulations.

Marian devotion, as portrayed in these texts, often mirrors the personal longing for unconditional love and acceptance. Through the lens of Marian imagery, authors delve into the psyche of their characters, unraveling the depths of human vulnerability and the innate desire for a maternal figure that can offer solace and understanding without judgment. The embodiment of Mary in literature becomes a bridge between humanity and the divine, facilitating a conversation that transcends the constraints of doctrinal orthodoxy.

Moreover, the depiction of Mary in Russian literature often carries with it a profound critique of societal structures. By elevating Mary as a symbol of pure, unconditional love, authors implicitly question the lack of compassion and empathy in their social milieu. It's as though through their Marian-inspired narratives, they beckon society to mirror the virtues of Mary in their everyday lives, promoting a culture of compassion, understanding, and selfless love.

One can't overlook the influence of Catholic Marian teachings in shaping these literary portrayals. The Catholic dogma of the

Immaculate Conception and the Assumption provide a doctrinal backdrop against which these literary depictions gain depth and meaning. By adopting and adapting these beliefs, Russian literature not only pays homage to Catholic Mariology but also enriches its own narrative landscapes with new symbols and meanings that resonate with universal themes of faith, hope, and love.

This confluence of Catholic and Russian spiritual narratives within the literary domain points to a deeper undercurrent of mutual influence and shared reverence. It's a dialogic exchange where theology and literature converse, debate, and enrich each other, revealing the intrinsic capability of art to transcend ecclesiastical divides and foster a communal spirit of devotion.

Ultimately, the Virgin Mary in Russian literature stands as a beacon of hope, a testament to the enduring power of maternal love as a universal touchstone for human aspiration and spiritual longing. In her, we find a convergence of the sacred and the profane, a nexus where human suffering meets divine compassion, a meeting point that continues to inspire and provoke, calling upon readers to explore the depths of their faith and humanity.

In concluding, the exploration of The Virgin Mary in Russian literature reveals not only the depth of Marian devotion but also its capacity to bridge diverse theological and cultural landscapes. This literary pilgrimage through the heart of Russian classics invites us to reconsider the role of Mary not merely as a religious figure but as a symbol of universal compassion and resilience amidst the human condition.

In academic discourse, such investigations pave the way for further interdisciplinary research, opening new vistas for understanding the interplay between doctrine and literature, faith and culture, especially in contexts that are seemingly dominated by differing theological traditions (Balthasar et al., 1990). As such, this chapter endeavours to contribute to the ongoing conversation about the presence of Catholicism in Russian literature, particularly through the lens of Marian devotion and symbolism.

Marian Devotion and Veneration

The veneration of the Virgin Mary, a pivotal aspect of Roman Catholicism, permeates Russian literature with a subtlety that belies its profound impact. This chapter explores the multifaceted role of Marian devotion in the works of Russian literary giants, elucidating how this reverence for Mary is not merely a religious act but a lens through which the complexities of faith, suffering, and redemption are examined. In the Russian literary canon, Mary's presence transcends her biblical role, embodying the quintessence of compassion, mercy, and maternal solace.

At the heart of Marian devotion in Russian literature is the concept of the Intercession of the Theotokos, a belief that the Virgin Mary intercedes on behalf of humanity to her Son, Jesus Christ. This theological premise underscores the literary portrayal of Mary as not only the Mother of God but as a celestial advocate for the sorrowful and the suffering. The writings of Dostoyevsky and Tolstoy, in particular, reflect a nuanced understanding of this intercessory power, often depicting characters who seek Mary's guidance and protection in moments of profound crisis.

Moreover, the veneration of Mary in these literary works serves to highlight the distinctly human need for compassionate understanding. Mary's role as a mediator between the divine and the human finds particular resonance in the context of Russian literature, where characters frequently grapple with existential despair and the thirst for spiritual redemption. Through Marian devotion, characters find a sanctuary, a source of unconditional love and understanding amidst their turmoil.

This literary motif of seeking refuge in Mary's compassion is emblematic of the broader thematic exploration of suffering and redemption in Russian literature. The Virgin Mary, in her immaculate sorrow and boundless mercy, is often portrayed as a beacon of hope for characters traversing the dark night of the soul. Her presence in these narratives reflects the Catholic understanding of Mary as a figure of solace and intercession, offering a glimpse of divine grace in the midst of human suffering.

The symbolic representation of Mary also extends to her role as the Mother of the Church, a dimension of Marian devotion that underscores the communal aspect of faith. In this context, Mary's embrace is not limited to the individual soul but encompasses the entire community of believers. The portrayal of Mary in Russian literature often echoes this communal aspect, highlighting her role in sustaining and nurturing the collective faith of the community.

Furthermore, the veneration of Mary in Russian literature is deeply intertwined with the theme of personal transformation. Characters inspired by Marian devotion frequently embark on journeys of self-discovery and spiritual awakening, with Mary serving as a guiding light on their path to redemption. This literary depiction resonates with the Catholic view of Mary as a model of virtue and holiness, encouraging believers to emulate her faith and humility.

It is important to note, however, that the embrace of Marian devotion in Russian literature is not a mere replication of Catholic dogma but a creative engagement with the complex tapestry of human emotion and spiritual longing. Russian writers, steeped in the Orthodox tradition, nevertheless articulate a vision of Mary that aligns with the universal human quest for meaning, love, and redemption.

In conclusion, the veneration of the Virgin Mary in Russian literature reflects a profound engagement with the mysteries of faith, suffering, and human redemption. Through the lens of Marian devotion, Russian writers explore the depths of the human condition, offering insights that resonate with the universal experiences of despair, hope, and the longing for divine grace. In this literary tradition, Mary emerges not only as a figure of religious veneration but as a symbol of the enduring quest for compassion, understanding, and spiritual renewal.

Intercessory Power and Compassion In the realm of Catholicism, as explored in the classic Russian literature of Dostoyevsky and Tolstoy, the concept of intercessory power and compassion emerges as a central theme. This theological principle illuminates the depths of human suffering, the pursuit of redemption, and the profound capacity for empathy amidst the harsh realities of existence. The Virgin Mary, embodying the pinnacle of these virtues, serves not only as a figure of devotional focus but also as a symbol of the ultimate intercessor, whose compassion and mercy are without bound.

The foundation of intercessory prayer within Catholicism hinges on the belief in the communal nature of the church, the mystical body of Christ. This theological framework posits that saints, particularly the Virgin Mary, can intercede on behalf of individuals, pleading for divine mercy and grace. This notion underscores a profound connectivity between the divine and the human, catalyzed by an unending stream of compassion channeled through the intercessors.

In Russian literature, this concept finds its expression through characters and narratives that mirror the transformative power of intercessory prayer and compassion. Characters besought by deep internal turmoil and external adversities often find solace in the compassion of others, echoing the intercessory role of the Virgin Mary. Herein lies a powerful dialogue between the divine and the mundane, mediated by figures of compassion who bear the weight of others' sufferings, offering solace and hope.

The embodiment of compassion in these literary works does not merely serve as a plot device; it challenges the reader to grapple with the philosophical and ethical dimensions of empathy. The narratives compel one to consider the ramifications of a life lived in the absence of compassion, contrasted with one illuminated by its presence. This dichotomy not only enriches the narrative depth but also aligns with the Catholic vision of a life steeped in virtuous living.

Intercessory prayer and compassion, particularly through the Virgin Mary, underscore a universal longing for an intermediary who understands human frailty and intercedes with unconditional love. This longing is magnified in the context of Russian literature, where characters often navigate the tumultuous seas of doubt, despair, and redemption. The intercessor emerges as a beacon of hope, guiding the wayward back to a path of moral and spiritual rectitude.

The narratives of Dostoyevsky and Tolstoy are replete with instances where the downtrodden and the derelict find redemption through acts of compassion, often inspired by or likened to Marian intercession. These moments illuminate the profound impact of empathy, highlighting its capacity to transcend the boundaries of the individual self, reaching out in a web of interconnectedness that binds humanity.

This concept also finds its resonance in the sacramental life of the church, where acts of mercy are both spiritual and corporeal. The literature delves into these acts, portraying them not only as moral imperatives but as manifestations of the divine presence in the world. Through these acts, characters often encounter the transformative power of grace, akin to the experience of intercessory prayer.

Moreover, the compassion exemplified by Marian intercession in literature serves as a catalyst for personal transformation. Characters are often led to a moment of epiphany, a realization of the need for grace, forgiveness, and the salvific power of compassion. This mirrors the Catholic understanding of conversion as a journey back to God, facilitated by the intercession of the saints and the Virgin Mary.

Yet, the exploration of Marian intercession in Russian literature also underscores the complexity of divine mercy. It invites a contemplation of the mystery of suffering, the role of free will, and the nature of redemption. These themes are woven into the fabric of the narratives, challenging both characters and readers to ponder the depth of God's love and the breadth of His mercy.

In conclusion, the exploration of intercessory power and compassion, particularly through the lens of Marian devotion, offers a rich tapestry of themes in Russian literature influenced by Catholicism. It brings to light the interconnectedness of human experience, the profound need for empathy, and the transformative power of divine intercession. Through this exploration, one gains insights into the depths of the human heart, the complexities of faith, and the enduring hope for redemption that characterizes the human condition.

The Mother as a Symbol of the Church

In the vast canon of Russian literature, the figure of the mother stands as a towering symbol of care, sacrifice, and unconditional love, mirroring the Church's spiritual role in the believers' lives. This representation is not by accident but a reflection of deeply ingrained theological parallels that find resonance in the narratives crafted by Russia's literary giants. Through the eyes of these characters and the vicissitudes of their lives, one can glimpse the Catholic Church's maternal qualities, offering sanctuary, guidance, and intercession much like a mother does for her child.

The symbolism of the Virgin Mary as the Mother of the Church is a vital component of Catholic theology, encapsulating the nurturing and protective role of the Church over its faithful. This notion is deftly woven into the fabric of Russian literature, where the maternal figure often becomes a conduit for the exploration of spiritual concepts and the human connection to the divine. The maternal archetype provides a tangible manifestation of the Church's abstract theological principles, making them accessible to the reader's empathy and understanding.

In literature, the portrayal of mother figures encompasses a spectrum of experiences and characteristics, each shedding light on different facets of the Church's role. The suffering mother, enduring pain and hardship for the sake of her children, mirrors the Church's sacrificial love for humanity, echoing the Passion of Christ. This motif not only highlights the depth of maternal and divine love but also serves as a model for the believers' own path of suffering and redemption.

Moreover, the guiding role of the mother, who leads her children through the complexities of life with wisdom and grace, finds its parallel in the Church's mission to shepherd the faithful towards spiritual enlightenment and goodness. This literary depiction underscores the Church's function as both teacher and protector, guiding its congregation through moral and ethical dilemmas in the pursuit of a righteous life.

Another compelling aspect is the intercessory power attributed to both the mother and the Church. Just as a mother intercedes on behalf of her children, seeking their welfare and defending them against harm, the Church intercedes for the faithful, mediating between the human and divine realms. This intercessory role is celebrated and venerated, affirming the belief in the Church's efficacy in spiritual affairs and its capacity to invoke divine mercy and grace.

Central to these literary portrayals is the concept of unyielding faith and trust in the maternal figure, echoing the trust bestowed upon the Church by the faithful. Characters often find themselves returning to their mothers, and symbolically to the Church, in times of crisis, seeking refuge and solace. This motif resonates with the Prodigal Son's return, highlighting the theme of forgiveness, mercy, and unconditional acceptance.

The figure of the mother also serves as a symbol of unity and community, embodying the Church's role in bringing together the faithful in a shared bond of love and compassion. In Russian literature, familial and community bonds are often framed around the central figure of the mother, reflecting the Church's communal aspect as the Body of Christ, where each member is connected through love and mutual support.

Furthermore, the motif of the mother as a bearer of life and nurturer of spiritual growth parallels the Church's life-giving sacraments, which sustain and nourish the believer's soul. In literary narratives, the actions of the mother often result in significant transformations, mirroring the transformative power of the sacraments and the Church's role in facilitating personal and communal renewal.

In conclusion, Russian literature provides a rich tapestry of maternal imagery, offering profound insights into the Catholic conception of the Church as a nurturing, guiding, and intercessory maternal entity. These narratives serve not only as cultural artifacts but also as theological reflections that embrace and elucidate key aspects of Catholic doctrine. Through the lens of literature, readers are invited to explore the depths of the Church's maternal dimension, fostering a deeper appreciation for its role in the spiritual life of humanity.

The Influence of Catholic Mysticism

The exploration of Catholic mysticism within the contours of classic Russian literature unveils a rich tapestry of spiritual inquiry and existential depth. This chapter delves into the ways in which Catholic mysticism, with its emphasis on personal encounters with the Divine and the pursuit of transcendence, permeates the works of Russian literary giants. While the Russian Orthodox Church dominantly shaped the religious and cultural landscape, the mystical currents of Catholicism carved out a significant, albeit less visible, niche influencing pivotal literary narratives.

The presence of mystical themes in Russian literature can be seen as a reflection of the universal human longing for an immediate and transformative encounter with the Divine. It's in the silence of the heart that authors like Dostoyevsky and Tolstoy found the language of mysticism, a language steeped in the traditions of Catholic contemplative practices. This deep inner journey towards the Divine is characterized by a movement away from the external and towards an intimate communion with God, mirroring the Catholic mystical tradition's pursuit of a direct experience of God's presence. Scholars argue that this mystical dimension adds a layer of complexity to the character's spiritual quests, enriching the narrative with both the struggles and the joys of seeking the Divine (Givens, 2018).

Moreover, the influence of Catholic mysticism is evident in the emphasis on contemplation found within Russian literature. This contemplative stance is often depicted through characters who withdraw from the world to engage in deep, reflective thought or prayer, seeking to transcend the material and connect with a higher reality. This mirrors the Catholic mystical tradition, where contemplation is seen as a fundamental means of encountering the Divine, fostering a profound sense of unity with God (Brown, 2020). Through these literary depictions, authors navigate the intricacies of human consciousness and spirituality, echoing the Catholic call to seek God within the innermost depths.

In grappling with the mystical, Russian literature frequently explores the concept of the transcendental and ineffable nature of God. Characters are often portrayed in moments of ineffable mystical experiences that defy rational explanation but lead to profound transformations. Such moments reflect Catholic mysticism's assertion that the Divine transcends human language and understanding, and yet can be intimately known through personal experience. The depiction of these encounters challenges readers to consider the nature of spiritual knowledge and the possibility of experiencing God beyond the limits of human reason (Green, 1986).

In conclusion, the influence of Catholic mysticism in classic Russian literature invites readers into a dialogue with the Divine, characterized by a deep, contemplative engagement with the mystery of God's presence. While rooted in a specific religious tradition, these mystical elements speak to a broader human experience of spiritual longing, inviting all to consider the ways in which the Divine might be encountered in the depths of the human heart. It's this universal appeal that allows the mystical dimensions of Russian literature to transcend cultural and religious boundaries, resonating with a diverse audience of believers and seekers alike.

The Presence of the Mystical and Transcendent

In exploring the vast landscapes of Russian literature influenced by Roman Catholicism, one cannot overlook the ethereal fibers of mysticism that weave through the narratives of both Fyodor Dostoyevsky and Leo Tolstoy. The mystical and transcendent dimensions, deeply embedded within the Catholic tradition, serve not merely as thematic ornaments but as pivotal conduits for expressing the intangible, the ineffable, and the divine. It is within this realm that the human soul encounters the divine directly, unmediated by the rational intellect or the sensory experiences.

Mystical theology, a crucial aspect of Catholic spirituality, emphasizes a direct, personal experience with God, often transcending language and rational thought. This element of Catholicism resonates profoundly within Russian literature, poignantly illustrating the characters' quest for such experiences in a world steeped in existential dilemmas and spiritual crises. The profound yearning for a tangible connection with the divine reflects a core trait within the human spiritual odyssey, a theme masterfully depicted in the works of Dostoyevsky and Tolstoy.

Dostoyevsky, in particular, delves into the mystical through the inner battles of his characters, highlighting their struggle between faith and doubt, sanctity and sin. The mystical experiences depicted in his narratives often emerge at the pinnacle of suffering or moral crises, serving as a beacon of hope and a testament to the presence of a transcendent reality beyond the apparent chaos of the material world.

Similarly, Tolstoy's writings are suffused with a quest for the transcendent, albeit through a slightly different lens. His exploration of the mystical emphasizes the inner transformation that occurs when one encounters the divine within the self. Tolstoy's focus on the "Kingdom of God is within you" aligns with the Catholic mystical tradition, which holds that divine encounters are not necessarily external or dramatic revelations but often unfold within the depths of one's soul.

The narrative methodologies employed by Dostoyevsky and Tolstoy to convey these mystical experiences also merit attention. Through intricate character development, dialogue, and inner monologues, they immerse the reader into the psychological and spiritual dimensions of their characters, allowing for a vicarious experience of the mystical and transcendent. This narrative immersion is not dissimilar to the mystical journey itself, which demands a departure from the superficial layers of reality and a plunge into the profound depths of being.

Moreover, the presence of the mystical in their works often serves as a critique of the prevailing rationalist and materialist worldview, challenging the notion that the empirical is the sole domain of reality. By depicting characters and scenarios that transcend the limits of rational explanation, Dostoyevsky and Tolstoy affirm the existence of a higher, spiritual dimension that critically engages with and sometimes supersedes the empirical world.

The themes of suffering, redemption, and transformation are intricately linked with the mystical and transcendent in Russian literature influenced by Catholicism. These motifs not only reflect the theological contours of Catholic mysticism but also resonate with the universal human experience. The narrative portrayal of these themes offers a glimpse into the soul's journey towards the divine, marked by trials, epiphanies, and moments of profound insight.

Furthermore, the mystical and transcendent are not confined to the interior life of characters but also manifest in the sacramental and liturgical elements depicted in these narratives. The presence of sacred rituals, symbols, and sacraments underscores the permeation of the divine into the material, pointing to a reality where the mystical is not remote but intimately intertwined with the fabric of everyday life.

In addition, the dialogue between faith and reason, a central theme in Catholic mysticism, is vividly portrayed in the works of Dostoyevsky and Tolstoy. Through their characters' journeys, the authors explore the limits of human understanding and the point at which one must surrender to the mystery of faith. This theme aligns with the Catholic mystical tradition, which acknowledges the importance of reason but also its insufficiency in fully comprehending the divine mystery.

It is also important to note the influence of church fathers and mystics on the theological underpinnings of these literary works. The writings of St. Augustine, St. John of the Cross, and other mystics provide a rich theological reservoir from which Dostoyevsky and Tolstoy draw. Their influence is evident in the themes of divine love, the dark night of the soul, and the transformative power of grace that permeate Russian literature.

The philosophical dialogues and inner monologues that characterize much of the narrative structure in the works of Dostoyevsky and Tolstoy also reflect the introspective and contemplative nature of mystical theology. These literary devices allow for a deep exploration of existential questions and the human condition, highlighting the relentless search for meaning, purpose, and ultimately, God.

The mystical and transcendent elements in Russian literature informed by Catholicism not only enrich the narrative texture but also offer profound insights into the spiritual landscape of humanity. They reflect a deep-seated longing for connection with the divine, an acknowledgment of the limitations of human understanding, and a celebration of the mystery that lies at the heart of existence.

In conclusion, the presence of the mystical and transcendent in Russian literature serves as a testament to the enduring influence of Catholic mysticism on the human imagination. By weaving these elements into their narratives, Dostoyevsky and Tolstoy invite readers into a profound engagement with the spiritual dimension, encouraging a contemplative stance towards life and its mysteries. Through their literary artistry, they not only depict the spiritual odyssey of their characters but also offer a mirror for the reader's own spiritual journey.

Contemplation and the Encounter with the Divine

In exploring the depths of Roman Catholic mysticism as it influences classic Russian literature, one cannot overlook the intricate dance between contemplation and the divine encounter. Central to Catholic tradition, contemplation acts as a bridge to the mystical, where the soul's quietude meets the Divine's overwhelming presence.

The essence of contemplation, within the Catholic framework, is not merely an introspective exercise but a profound, meditative dialogue with God. This dialogue, silent and steeped in the heart's depths, pierces through the veil of the mundane to touch upon the transcendent. It is here, in this sacred exchange, that literature finds its most ethereal expressions of faith and mysticism.

Consider how contemplation, as a form of deep prayer and meditation, permeates the works of revered Russian authors. Though these authors may wrestle with the theological intricacies of Catholic doctrine, their narratives often reflect a quintessentially Catholic approach to encountering the divine: through the quiet, persistent pursuit of God in the stillness of one's heart.

This meditative approach to God is not merely about achieving personal enlightenment or inner peace. It's about a transformative encounter that reshapes the soul, aligns it with divine will, and propels it towards acts of love and mercy. Such transformation is vividly depicted in literature, where characters' contemplative experiences often lead to profound moral and spiritual revelations.

Consider the significance of the sacramental in this contemplative journey. Catholicism holds that grace is imparted through the sacraments, which, in turn, enrich one's capacity for divine encounters. Through narrative exploration, Russian literature frequently mirrors this sacramental journey, guiding characters (and readers) through their own transformative experiences of grace.

Moreover, the role of suffering within contemplative practice must be acknowledged. Catholic mysticism often views suffering as a pathway to deeper union with Christ, a concept that resonates deeply within Russian literary traditions. The characters' trials and tribulations become not mere narrative obstacles but crucibles for divine encounter and spiritual refinement.

It is within the silent, solitary moments of contemplation that characters come face to face with their own vulnerabilities, only to find God waiting in their fragility. This encounter is not one of despair but hope, illuminating the path to redemption and the possibility of divine grace.

The transformative power of these encounters often leads characters to a radical reorientation of their life. It is in the aftermath of divine touch that many find the impetus for moral courage, altruism, and a deeper, more authentic engagement with the world around them. This narrative motif not only reflects the mystical heart of Catholicism but also underscores literature's potential to inspire virtue in its readers.

The juxtaposition of divine transcendence and immanence within contemplative practice is another aspect vividly explored in literature. God is both beyond and intimately present within creation, a paradox that mysticism embraces and literature often seeks to encapsulate. Characters' contemplative journeys thus reflect this paradoxical encounter with a God who is wholly other yet deeply immanent.

Furthermore, community and communion play a critical role in this contemplative engagement. Though the encounter with the divine is deeply personal, Catholic mysticism situates this experience within the broader context of the Church's communal life. In literature, this is echoed through narratives that not only highlight individual encounters with God but also the way these encounters transform relationships, fostering a sense of spiritual solidarity and communal healing.

The influence of the Eucharistic celebration as the ultimate contemplative act and divine encounter cannot be overstated. In the Eucharist, the mystical body of Christ is made manifest, uniting heaven and earth in a moment of profound communion. This sacramental motif, with its deep roots in Catholic mysticism, finds echoes in literature where communal meals or moments of shared suffering often symbolize spiritual unity and divine presence.

In conclusion, the contemplative journey and the encounter with the divine, as articulated within Catholic mysticism, profoundly shape the thematic and moral landscape of Russian literature. Through the silent whispers of prayer and the tumultuous stirrings of the soul, characters navigate their spiritual odysseys, reflecting the broader human quest for meaning, connection, and ultimate communion with the Divine.

It's within this complex interplay of silence and revelation, suffering and grace, that the mystical heart of Catholicism beats most vividly in the pages of Russian literary masterpieces. The contemplative path, marked by an earnest seeking after God, offers readers not only a reflection of their spiritual longings but also a beacon of hope in the enduring promise of divine encounter and transformation.

Moral Theology in the Narratives

The exploration of moral theology within the variegated tapestry of Russian literature, especially in the works of its paragons, Dostoyevsky and Tolstoy, presents a compelling study of the intrinsic connection between narrative and doctrine. This chapter delves into how these narratives, woven with the threads of Catholic moral theology, illuminate the virtues of charity, the importance of personal conversion, and the impact of community. At the heart of these stories lies the profound understanding that the moral life is not merely about adherence to a set of rules or commands but is deeply entrenched in the complexities and struggles of the human experience.

In dissecting the virtue of charity and the works of mercy as espoused in these narratives, one encounters a staggering depth of insight into the nature of love as an essential moral good. Through the embodiment of these virtues in their characters, Dostoyevsky and Tolstoy not only underscore their importance but also highlight their transformative power. This reflection aligns closely with the Catholic emphasis on charity as foundational, a sentiment best encapsulated in the theological principle that "faith by itself, if it does not have works, is dead" (James 2:17). The interplay between faith and works within these stories serves as a vivid illustration of this truth, emphasizing that moral theology is not just theoretical but intimately connected with the practicalities of living a virtuous life.

The theme of personal conversion is another predominant thread in Russian literary narrative, portraying the journey from sin to redemption as both complex and nuanced. The process of conversion is depicted not as a singular event but as an ongoing journey, where characters grapple with their flaws, confront their sins, and strive towards a life of virtue. This resonates with the Catholic understanding of conversion as a lifelong process of turning towards God and away from sin. The narratives of Dostoyevsky and Tolstoy are replete with such journeys, illustrating the Catholic teaching that grace is always available to those who seek it, and that transformation is always possible, irrespective of one's past.

Furthermore, the role of community in these works cannot be understated. The narratives advocate for a moral theology that is deeply communal, reflecting the Catholic view that salvation and sanctification are not solely individual endeavors but are deeply entwined with others' lives. The characters' interactions and the communities they form are not merely backdrops for individual moral quests but are integral to the moral and spiritual development of the individuals themselves. This perspective highlights the interconnectedness of all people and the shared journey towards virtue and holiness.

Through the lens of Catholic moral theology, Dostoyevsky and Tolstoy's works offer profound insights into the human condition, the struggle for redemption, the importance of community, and the transformative power of love. Their narratives serve not only as a reflection of the moral complexities that define human existence but also as a testament to the enduring relevance of Catholic moral teaching in the pursuit of a good and meaningful life.

The Virtue of Charity and the Works of Mercy

The renditions of moral theology within the corpus of Russian literature notably pivot on the critical underpinnings of Catholic doctrine, with the virtue of charity and the works of mercy being chief among them. This focus does not merely serve as a narrative device but rather as a profound exploration into man's capacity for selflessness and divine grace. Within the context of these narratives, charity is often depicted not just as an act of giving, but as a transformative force, capable of altering the course of human lives and destinies.

At the heart of Catholic teaching, the virtue of charity holds a paramount position, emphasizing love for God above all and for neighbors as oneself. This principle, deeply ingrained in the fabric of Catholic moral theology, finds its echo in Russian literature, where characters are often confronted with the stark realities of poverty, injustice, and human suffering. In their respective journeys, they are called upon to perform the works of mercy, acts that are both corporal—feeding the hungry, sheltering the homeless, visiting the sick—and spiritual, such as counseling the doubtful and praying for the living and the dead (Catechism of the Catholic Church, 1994).

The narrative arcs woven by these literary giants often lead their protagonists through the crucible of suffering, only to emerge enlightened by the realization of the paramount significance of charity. It's in the dialogue between these personal revelations and the broader societal contexts that the moral theologies of Catholicism find their most potent expression. Characters' engagements in acts of mercy often serve as pivotal moments of conversion, not merely in a religious sense but in a profound, existential transformation that redefines their understanding of purpose and community.

Moreover, the portrayal of charity and the works of mercy in literature serves as an implicit critique of the societal structures of the time, highlighting the inadequacies and injustices that pervade the social fabric. It challenges the reader to not only empathize with the human condition but also to consider the imperative of charity as a foundational element of moral theology. This, in turn, beckons towards a personal call to action, an invitation to embody these virtues in the pursuit of a more just and compassionate society.

In conclusion, the exploration of charity and the works of mercy within the narratives of Russian literature transcends the boundaries of mere storytelling. It embodies a profound enquiry into the nature of human existence, moral responsibility, and the potential for redemption and transformation through acts of love. Such narratives underscore the timeless relevance of Catholic moral theology as a vehicle for understanding and navigating the complexities of the human condition, offering both a critique and a compass for the moral and spiritual journey.

Personal Conversion and Community The mosaic of human experience, as depicted in classic Russian literature, is profoundly impacted by the interplay between personal conversion and the broader fabric of community. This dynamic interaction, vital to the understanding of Catholic influences within the genre, reveals the inherent tension and harmony between individual transformation and communal life.

Personal conversion, a cornerstone of Catholic teaching, is not merely an inward-looking process. It involves a radical reorientation of one's entire being towards the divine, which, by its nature, has implications far beyond the individual. It echoes the call to be a 'light to the world,' serving as a beacon of change within one's immediate surroundings. The transformative power of personal conversion extends beyond the boundaries of the self, fostering a communal spirituality that underpins societal values and norms.

In the realm of Russian literature, this theme of conversion and its communal repercussions is pervasive. Characters often undergo profound spiritual awakenings, leading them to challenge and, in turn, be challenged by their communities. This literary exploration mirrors the Catholic understanding that personal faith must be lived out within the body of the Church and the wider world, advocating a faith that is both deeply personal and inherently social.

The idea that one's conversion could act as a catalyst for communal transformation is a testament to the interconnectedness of human relationships. It speaks to the notion that individual actions of faith and morality ripple through the social fabric, contributing to the communal pursuit of the common good. The Catholic Church posits that true conversion encompasses a commitment to social justice and the welfare of others, recognizing that personal sanctity is incomplete without its expression in works of charity and mercy.

This synthesis between individual and community is vividly portrayed in the narratives of both Dostoyevsky and Tolstoy. Characters frequently face moral dilemmas that compel them to act in ways that resonate with, or revolt against, societal norms. These literary moments underscore the complex dialogue between the inner moral compass of the individual and the collective ethos of their community.

The process of personal conversion is often marked by suffering and sacrifice—a theme that resonates with Catholic soteriology. The path to personal sanctification and the betterment of the community is seldom easy or straightforward. It is fraught with trials that test the resilience of faith and the depth of one's commitment to societal transformation. Through their protagonists, Russian authors delve into the paradox that personal redemption and community upliftment are often achieved through suffering and self-denial.

The communal aspect of conversion is also reflected in the Catholic concept of the 'communion of saints.' This doctrine emphasizes the spiritual solidarity between the faithful on earth, the souls in purgatory, and the saints in heaven. It suggests that personal sanctity has implications that transcend time and space, influencing the wider community across generations. This timeless and transcendent aspect of community is mirrored in the enduring impact of character transformations in Russian literature, which often serve as moral and spiritual landmarks within the narrative.

In juxtaposing Catholic doctrines with the narratives of Russian literature, it becomes evident that personal conversion cannot be divorced from its communal implications. The journey of faith is both an individual and a collective endeavor, wherein the transformation of the self invariably implicates the transformation of others. The portrayal of this dynamic in literature not only enriches the narrative complexity but also offers a profound commentary on the human condition.

The interaction between personal conversion and community in Russian literature underscores the dialogic nature of faith. It highlights how personal belief is continually shaped and reshaped in the crucible of community life. This ongoing dialogue between the self and society reflects the Catholic vision of the Church as the living body of Christ, evolving and adapting in response to the spiritual needs and realities of its members.

Furthermore, the theme accentuates the role of the Church not merely as a spiritual refuge for individuals but as a transformative force within society. It underlines the Church's mission to not only save souls but to uplift communities, advocating for justice, peace, and the integral development of people. This mission, vividly captured in literature, demonstrates the inextricable link between personal transformation and social action.

The dynamic interplay between personal conversion and community invites readers to reflect on the role of faith in the public sphere. It challenges prevailing notions of religion as a private affair, advocating instead for a faith that is active, engaged, and outward-looking. It reinforces the idea that one's spiritual journey is intimately connected with their social and moral responsibilities to others.

In conclusion, the examination of personal conversion and its communal implications within classic Russian literature offers invaluable insights into the Catholic understanding of faith in action. It reveals that the personal journey of faith is inextricably linked with the collective journey towards a more just, compassionate, and holy community. This intertwining of the individual and the communal in the pursuit of sanctity and social justice reflects the heart of Catholic teaching and underscores the profound impact of Catholicism on Russian literature.

The Church Militant and the Church Triumphant

In the tapestry of classic Russian literature, particularly the works that are steeped in Catholic doctrine, a vivid depiction of the cosmic struggle between good and evil emerges. This chapter embarks on an exploration of how this eternal battle, delineated through the Church Militant and the Church Triumphant, is mirrored in the lives of characters, shaping their narratives and, by extension, the moral and spiritual dimensions of their world.

The Church Militant, which represents the faithful on Earth engaged in the spiritual battle against sin, the devil, and his malevolent forces, finds a potent expression in Russian literature. Characters are often depicted as soldiers of faith, embroiled in a relentless fight against their own vices and the temptations of a corrupt world. It's a motif that underscores the tumultuous journey of the soul towards purity and salvation, capturing the essence of the human condition as viewed through a Catholic lens.

Equally compelling is the portrayal of the Church Triumphant — the saints and angels in Heaven who have overcome the world and now share in God's glory. This concept illuminates the narrative potential of eternal reward, offering solace and a promise of victory for the righteous. The communion of saints, in particular, serves as a beacon of hope for characters navigating the treacherous waters of sin and redemption.

This dichotomy between the militant and the triumphant aspects of the Church not only enriches the spiritual landscape of Russian literature but also offers insight into the Catholic worldview. The battle against evil is not an external or mythical conflict but a deeply personal endeavor that unfolds within the heart of each believer. Russian authors adeptly weave these themes into their works, presenting the spiritual journey as an arduous path that eventually leads to triumph through grace and perseverance.

In delving into the lives of characters embroiled in spiritual warfare, one cannot help but discern the influence of Catholic theology on the narrative arc. The concepts of sin, struggle, and salvation manifest not only in their actions but in their profound inner monologues. These reflective passages expose the soul's vulnerability to temptation and its capacity for divine grace, echoing the Church's teachings on the necessity of vigilance and prayer in the life of the believer.

The communion of saints stands out as a particularly evocative symbol, uniting the Church Militant with the Church Triumphant. In these literary works, the saints do not merely occupy a distant, celestial realm but actively intercede for those on Earth, guiding and comforting them. This aspect of Catholic doctrine emphasizes the interconnectedness of all members of the Church, offering a model of spiritual solidarity and support that transcends the boundaries of life and death.

Moreover, the portrayal of these themes is instrumental in highlighting the transformative power of faith. Characters who engage in the spiritual battle often emerge profoundly changed, their journeys reflecting the process of conversion and sanctification. The narrative trajectory from sin to redemption mirrors the Church's message of hope and the possibility of new life in Christ.

By integrating the concepts of the Church Militant and the Church Triumphant into their narratives, Russian authors illuminate the moral and spiritual struggles of their characters, while also engaging with the broader theological debates of their time. This dynamic interplay between literature and doctrine not only enriches the literary canon but also offers profound insights into the human quest for meaning and salvation.

In conclusion, the chapters of Russian literature that delve into the cosmic battle between good and evil serve as a testament to the enduring influence of Catholicism. Through the vivid portrayal of the Church Militant and the Church Triumphant, authors weave a rich tapestry of faith, struggle, and redemption that continues to resonate with readers across generations and cultures.

The Battle Against Evil

The narrative of the spiritual battle against evil, a theme deeply embedded in the heart of Catholic doctrine, finds its resonance within the pages of classic Russian literature, presenting itself with a fierceness and complexity that begs for an understanding beyond the superficial. At its core, this battle is not merely a confrontation between good and evil entities but interweaves the human experience with divine aspirations, thereby illuminating the intricate paths of the human soul towards redemption and sanctification. The Church Militant, in its relentless struggle against the forces of darkness, embodies this earthly journey, marked by trials, tribulations, and the constant pursuit of virtue in the face of sin.

These themes are prevalent in the works of Russian literary giants who, knowingly or not, wove the fundamental tenets of Catholic spirituality into their narratives. Through their characters and plots, they explored the depths of the human condition, the potency of sin, and the luminal spaces wherein lies the possibility for repentance and the grace of conversion. Characters are often depicted as embroiled in the throes of existential crises, emblematic of the spiritual warfare waged within the soul, mirroring the Church's teachings on the necessity of perseverance, prayer, and reliance on divine aid in the fight against evil.

The concept of spiritual warfare, as elucidated by the Church, posits that the Christian life is a battle, a continuous struggle against evil within and without. This axiom finds expression in literature through characters who confront their inner demons, societal decay, and the overt temptations of an antagonistic world. Their victories and defeats serve to highlight the Church's assertion that faith, hope, and love are the weapons with which this war is fought, and that through Christ, victory is assured (Vatican II, Lumen Gentium).

Moreover, the sacraments and sacramentals, pivotal in sustaining the believer's resolve in this battle, are subtly mirrored in the rituals and symbols that permeate these literary works. The act of confession, the Eucharist, and the veneration of saints and relics find echoes in the pivotal moments of decision, transformation, and intercession that define the narrative arcs of key protagonists. These elements serve to underscore the indissoluble link between the physical and spiritual realms, and the power of divine grace to conquer sin and death.

The portrayal of evil in these narratives is multifaceted, reflecting the Church's teachings on the nature of sin and its repercussions. Evil is not merely an external adversary but is often depicted as emanating from within the human heart, a byproduct of free will turned away from God. This nuanced understanding of evil underscores the complexity of the moral and spiritual dilemmas faced by characters, and by extension, the reader, urging a contemplation of one's own spiritual state and the universal call to conversion.

Central to Catholic eschatology and indeed, the literature that it inspires, is the belief in the final victory over evil, a theme that resonates profoundly in the portrayal of characters' ultimate destinies. The Church Triumphant symbolizes the culmination of the battle against evil, a vision of heavenly glory where saints, having won their earthly battles, partake in the Beatific Vision. This eschatological hope permeates the narratives, offering a glimpse of redemption and the promise of a new creation, free from the shackles of sin and death, where righteousness dwells.

In essence, the battle against evil, as depicted in Russian literature influenced by Catholic thought, serves as a microcosm of the cosmic struggle between good and evil, encapsulated within the human experience. It prompts a reflection on the role of free will in the salvation narrative, the necessity of divine grace, and the indomitable spirit of humanity in its quest for the divine.

Ultimately, these literary explorations offer not only a rich tableau of human struggle and divine providence but also serve as a testament to the enduring relevance of Catholic spiritual and moral teachings in addressing the perennial questions of good and evil, sin and redemption, death and eternal life. In doing so, they enrich our understanding of the human condition, the nature of God, and the path to sanctity, echoing the Church's mission to guide souls to their heavenly home.

Through the lens of Russian literature, the battle against evil unveils the profound dialogues between faith and doubt, sanctity and sin, despair and hope. It reveals the unyielding power of love to overcome darkness, a theme that lies at the heart of both Catholic doctrine and the human saga. As such, it invites readers to embark on their own spiritual journey, armed with the insights gleaned from these literary and theological reflections, towards the ultimate triumph of good over evil, in accordance with divine will.

In conclusion, the exploration of the battle against evil through the doctrinal and narrative lens of the Church Militant and the Church Triumphant uncovers the intertwined destinies of humanity and the divine, a journey marked by conflict, redemption, and the promise of eternal victory. This journey, as reflected in the annals of Russian literature, continues to inspire, challenge, and invite contemplation on the mysteries of faith, the power of grace, and the final victory of love.

Spiritual Warfare in the Lives of Characters The exploration of spiritual warfare within the depths of Russian literature, especially through the lens of Catholicism, uncovers a rich tapestry of internal and external battles faced by characters. This sub-section delves into the multifaceted dimensions of spiritual warfare as manifested in the work of canonical authors like Dostoyevsky and Tolstoy, and how these narratives resonate with the Catholic understanding of the struggle between good and evil. In these stories, spiritual warfare is not merely a backdrop but a central theme that drives characters to profound existential crises, moments of revelation, and ultimately, decisions that define their moral trajectory.

The concept of spiritual warfare, as understood in Catholicism, involves the battle for the human soul fought between divine forces and malevolent entities. This battle, while invisible, manifests through temptations, sufferings, and the moral choices individuals face. In Russian literature, this is vividly depicted through characters who encounter intense spiritual dilemmas, torn between their passions and the pursuit of holiness. Dostoyevsky's narratives, for instance, often portray characters who undergo profound inner turmoil, wrestling with questions of faith, doubt, and redemption.

In the case of Alyosha Karamazov from "The Brothers Karamazov," the struggle of spiritual warfare is palpable in his journey. Alyosha's faith is tested through his interactions with his family and the broader societal challenges of his time. The internal battle he faces, mirrored in the external chaos surrounding him, highlights the constant presence of spiritual warfare in the pursuit of righteousness and truth. It's a testament to Alyosha's character that despite the cacophony of existential challenges, his faith remains unwavering—an exemplar of the victory in spiritual warfare achieved through grace and steadfast belief in the goodness of God.

Similarly, Tolstoy's "War and Peace" reveals spiritual warfare through its treatment of human suffering and the pursuit of spiritual peace amidst the ravages of conflict. Characters such as Prince Andrei and Pierre Bezukhov exemplify the internal struggle between despair and hope, cynicism and faith. Through their journeys, Tolstoy crafts a narrative that echoes the Catholic understanding of spiritual warfare—emphasizing the significance of internal transformation and the power of divine grace in overcoming the spiritual malaise that war and suffering bring.

In examining these characters and themes, one cannot overlook the sacramental aspects that underpin the notion of spiritual warfare in Catholicism. Confession, penance, and the Eucharist emerge within these narratives as means for the characters to confront and combat the forces of evil besieging them.

Dostoyevsky, in particular, utilizes the sacrament of confession as a critical juncture for characters to confront their sins and seek redemption, thereby engaging directly with the aspect of spiritual warfare concerned with the reconciliation of the soul with God.

Moreover, the virulent struggle against demonic influences is a recurring motif in Russian literature that starkly reflects the Catholic understanding of spiritual warfare. Characters often face encounters with tangible representations of evil, sometimes in their own psyche, which illuminates the perennial battle between good and evil taking place within the human heart. Through these encounters, authors reveal the fragile boundaries separating sanctity from sinfulness, and the perpetual effort required to align one's life with divine will.

The role of the Virgin Mary and the saints as intercessors in spiritual warfare is another dimension explored in Russian literature, resonating with Catholic teachings. Characters often experience moments of Marian devotion or seek the intercession of saints in moments of acute spiritual crisis, invoking the "Church triumphant" as allies in their battle against sin and temptation. This thematic element underscores the communal and intercessory aspect of spiritual warfare, highlighting the Catholic belief in the communion of saints and the powerful role of the Virgin Mary as protectress and mediator.

Furthermore, the concept of personal conversion and transformation holds a central place in the narrative arc of characters embroiled in spiritual warfare. The journey from sin to repentance, and ultimately to sanctity, is a path fraught with obstacles and temptations. Yet, it is also a journey illuminated by grace and the possibility of redemption. In this, Russian literature presents a deeply Catholic understanding of spiritual warfare, not as an insurmountable battle, but as a transformative process that draws the soul closer to God and to the ultimate victory over evil.

It's noteworthy that the depiction of spiritual warfare in Russian literature does not shy away from the complexities and paradoxes of the human condition. In fact, it delves deeply into the ambiguity of moral choices, the possibility of grace in moments of despair, and the coexistence of doubt and faith within the human heart. These narratives mirror the Catholic viewpoint that spiritual warfare is a nuanced and multifaceted struggle, requiring not just resistance to evil, but also a proactive pursuit of virtue and the common good.

The efficacy of prayer as a weapon in spiritual warfare is yet another aspect brilliantly woven into the fabric of Russian literary narratives. Prayer emerges not merely as a ritualistic practice but as a profound dialogue with the divine, offering characters strength, guidance, and solace amidst their trials. This reflects the Catholic understanding of prayer as a vital element in the battle against spiritual desolation and as a means of sustaining the soul's journey towards God.

In conclusion, the portrayal of spiritual warfare in the lives of characters in Russian literature provides a rich and nuanced exploration of the Catholic spiritual tradition. Through their narratives, authors like Dostoyevsky and Tolstoy offer insights into the myriad ways individuals confront and overcome the forces of evil, armed with faith, grace, and the support of the heavenly hosts. These stories not only entertain but also illuminate the path of spiritual warfare, guiding readers towards a deeper understanding of the ongoing battle for the human soul and the promise of redemption that lies at its heart.

The Communion of Saints

In exploring the profound depths of the Church Militant and the Church Triumphant, one must necessarily encounter the doctrine of the Communion of Saints, a tenet that transcends not only the boundaries of heaven and earth but also deeply entwines the human spirit with the divine. This notion, rooted in the rich soil of Catholic theology, finds its branches reaching into the heart of Russian literature, offering a unique lens through which to view the works of its most esteemed authors.

At its core, the Communion of Saints is a doctrine that professes the solidarity between all members of the Christian community, the living and the dead, the saints in heaven, souls in purgatory, and the faithful on earth. It's a spiritual union that defies the constraints of time and space, bonded by a shared participation in the sacraments and, most importantly, in the Eucharistic celebration. This unity is manifest in the belief that saints, with their proximity to God, can intercede on behalf of humanity, bridging the chasm between the finite and the infinite (Catechism of the Catholic Church, 1994).

The narrative works of Dostoyevsky and Tolstoy are imbued with this mystical communion, though their approaches and interpretations diverge significantly. In Dostoyevsky's universe, the Communion of Saints permeates the fabric of existence, where characters are often shown to be interconnected in their suffering and redemption, mirroring the intercessory role of saints. This is not merely a theological proposition but a palpable, lived reality that influences the destinies of his characters.

Furthermore, Dostoyevsky's exploration of suffering, shared among his characters, reflects a deeply Catholic understanding of redemptive suffering. It signifies a collective journey toward sanctity, where each individual's tribulations contribute to the sanctification of the whole, thereby embodying the essence of the Communion of Saints. This perspective underscores the belief that no soul is isolated in its suffering or its salvation, but is part of an intricate web of spiritual kinship.

In contrast, Tolstoy's engagement with the concept of spiritual communion is more nuanced, often critiquing institutional religion while still portraying a profound connectedness among individuals. Despite his skepticism towards formal religious practices, Tolstoy champions the ethical imperatives of love and nonviolence, principles that echo the fundamental tenets of the Communion of Saints. In his narratives, this communion is realized through acts of love, forgiveness, and mutual support among his characters, suggesting that the divine can be manifested in the bonds of human solidarity.

The shared suffering and quest for redemption, presented by both Dostoyevsky and Tolstoy, not only highlight the theological richness of the Communion of Saints but also reveal a profound understanding of human nature. It suggests an intrinsic desire for connection, both spiritually and materially, acknowledging that individual salvation is inextricably linked to the collective well-being of the community.

This exploration of the Communion of Saints in Russian literature invites readers to reflect on the interconnectedness of humanity and the divine, urging a reconsideration of the boundaries that separate the sacred from the profane. It beckons us to recognize the saints among us and within us, guiding us towards a more holistic understanding of salvation and sanctity.

The intercession of saints, as portrayed in these narratives, is not a mere theological abstraction but a tangible, lived experience. Through their intercessions, the saints offer guidance, hope, and a model of sanctity that transcends earthly limitations, thus embodying the true spirit of the Communion of Saints. This portrayal not only enriches the theological landscape of Russian literature but also provides a beacon of light for readers navigating the complexities of faith and morality.

The doctrine of the Communion of Saints, therefore, serves as a foundational element in the spiritual and moral framework of Russian literature, demonstrating the enduring influence of Catholicism on its narrative and philosophical dimensions. It encapsulates a vision of the world where the divine permeates the mundane, where the veil between heaven and earth is lifted, revealing the intricate tapestry of spiritual kinship that binds us all.

As we delve deeper into the works of Dostoyevsky and Tolstoy, we are invited to contemplate the myriad ways in which the Communion of Saints manifests itself. Whether through the shared suffering of characters, their quest for redemption, or the acts of love that bind them, this doctrine offers a potent lens through which to interpret their literary and theological significance.

In conclusion, the Communion of Saints occupies a pivotal place in the intersection of Catholicism and Russian literature, providing a profound commentary on the nature of spiritual connectedness. It challenges us to transcend the limitations of our individualistic perspectives, inviting us into a communal journey towards salvation and sanctity. Thus, it remains a testament to the enduring legacy of faith in the literary imagination, offering insights that resonate with the depths of the human condition.

Chapter 12: Eschatology: Concepts of Heaven and Hell

In delving into the eschatological framework that underpins much of classic Russian literature, particularly within the works influenced by Roman Catholicism, it becomes essential to untangle the nuanced interpretations of heaven and hell. These concepts serve not only as metaphysical destinations but also as integral ciphers through which the moral and spiritual consequences of human actions are decoded. Within the Catholic tradition, heaven and hell are understood as the ultimate realms of reward and punishment, respectively, echoing the dualities of divine justice and mercy. This dichotomy finds a vivid canvas in the narrative structures of Dostoyevsky's and Tolstoy's masterpieces, where characters are often depicted at the crossroads of salvation and damnation, wrestling with choices that bear eternal significance.

The portrayal of afterlife in these literatures encourages a profound contemplation on the nature of personal judgment and the hope for universal salvation. Heaven is depicted not merely as an end but as a beacon that guides the moral compass of humanity, offering a vision of eternal peace and communion with the divine. Conversely, hell emerges as the shadow cast by human failings, a realm where the absence of love and grace underscores the ultimate tragedy of separation from God. Through these narrative explorations, the texts invite reflection on the broader theological assertion that every soul's destiny hinges upon free will, moral integrity, and the possibility of redemption through God's unbounded mercy (Catechism of the Catholic Church, 1993).

Ultimately, the exploration of eschatological themes in Russian literature serves to illuminate the profound moral and spiritual inquiries at the heart of human experience. It reflects a deep engagement with the Catholic eschatological vision, where the concepts of heaven and hell transcend mere doctrinal abstractions to become vivid landscapes upon which the drama of human salvation unfolds. This interplay between narrative and theology opens up rich avenues for understanding the complexities of faith, redemption, and the quest for meaning in the mortal coil, echoing the enduring dialogue between Catholicism and Russian literary tradition.

Afterlife as the Ultimate Justice

In the tapestry of human existence, where the threads of moral complexity are woven with the fibers of spiritual longing, the concept of the afterlife stands as an eternal testament to the notion of ultimate justice. The belief that deeds, both good and bad, find their reckoning beyond the mortal realm, encapsulates the essence of Catholic doctrine and has been a profound influence on the moral and existential themes present in classic Russian literature. It's within this belief system that the afterlife serves not merely as a destination but as a divine court, where the scales of justice are balanced with an unerring precision that mortal jurisprudence can only aspire to.

This understanding of the afterlife, as more than just a continuation of existence but as the culmination of a soul's moral journey, informs the narrative arcs and character developments within the works of Dostoyevsky and Tolstoy. Characters are depicted in the throes of moral conflict, where their choices are weighed down by the spiritual implications of the afterlife. The notion that every action carries with it a consequence that transcends tangible reality imbues their literary worlds with a palpable tension, where the specter of eternal judgment looms large over every decision.

The Catholic emphasis on confession, penance, and redemption further nuances this portrayal of the afterlife as the ultimate form of justice. Within this framework, the confessional acts as the crucible in which the soul is purified, enabling even the most errant sinner to find salvation. This transformative process underscores the belief in a merciful judge who seeks not to condemn but to redeem, offering a path to salvation that is fraught with moral complexity but ultimately accessible to all who seek it with genuine contrition.

However, it is essential to consider the impact of such theological concepts on the human psyche. The belief in an afterlife where ultimate justice is meted out serves as both a warning and a source of solace. It warns against the complacency of moral relativism, asserting that actions have consequences beyond their immediate outcomes. Simultaneously, it offers solace to those who suffer, providing a cosmic assurance that injustices endured in this life will be rectified in the next. This dual aspect of the afterlife as the ultimate justice reflects the Catholic understanding of God's nature as both infinitely just and infinitely merciful.

In the final analysis, the Catholic conception of the afterlife as a place of ultimate justice profoundly impacts the ethical and existential underpinnings of Russian literature. It is a doctrine that at once elevates and terrifies, offering a vision of the world where every soul stands accountable and yet, paradoxically, every soul is offered a path to redemption. The intricate balance between justice and mercy, retribution and forgiveness, forms a critical backdrop against which the dramas of Dostoyevsky and Tolstoy unfold, providing a rich tapestry of moral and spiritual inquiry that continues to resonate with readers across time and space.

Personal Judgment and Universal Salvation

In the exploration of the eternal themes of Catholicism as they intersect with classic Russian literature, the nuanced concepts of personal judgment and universal salvation emerge as profound elements worthy of examination. Catholic theology posits that each soul faces personal judgment at the moment of death, accounting for the deeds of a lifetime, and yet, it also entertains the hopeful doctrine of universal salvation—the ultimate reconciliation of all souls with God. This tension between individual accountability and collective redemption forms a captivating backdrop to the narratives crafted by Dostoyevsky and Tolstoy, as they wrestle with the bounds of divine justice and mercy.

The Catholic understanding of personal judgment asserts that upon death, each individual is judged immediately by God. This judgment dictates the soul's further passage into Heaven, Purgatory, or Hell. Herein lies a crucial question that Russian literature often seeks to address: What role does personal responsibility play in our spiritual destiny? Through their characters' trials and moral dilemmas, these Russian authors probe the depths of human freedom and culpability, reflecting Catholicism's emphasis on the moral weight of personal choices.

Conversely, the hope for universal salvation represents a merciful counterpart to the solemnity of personal judgment. This is the hope that, in the fullness of time, God's unbounded love and mercy will extend to every soul, offering a pathway to reconciliation for all. Such a concept challenges the boundaries of human understanding of justice, pushing the reader towards a more expansive conception of divine love. This theological perspective underscores many narrative arcs in Russian literature, where the most fallen characters often embark on journeys toward redemption, suggesting an undercurrent of universal salvific hope.

Through the lens of Catholic theology, the interplay of these doctrines raises compelling considerations about the nature of God's justice. Is divine judgment the final word on a soul's fate, or is there always a possibility for mercy and redemption? Russian novels often embody this debate, setting the stage for deep theological inquiry through the lives of their characters. For instance, characters that seem beyond redemption find paths to salvation, echoing the Catholic teaching of God's infinite mercy and the hope for universal reconciliation.

Moreover, the portrayal of Purgatory in these literatures—a state of purification for souls destined for Heaven but still needing to atone for their sins—highlights the Catholic doctrine of mercy within judgment. This state reflects a profound understanding of human imperfection and the compassionate patience of divine justice, themes deeply rooted in the personal struggles of characters found in Russian classics.

It is also imperative to consider how the concept of free will intersects with these doctrines. Catholicism holds that God grants humans the freedom to choose their paths, making personal judgment a reflection of one's life choices in accordance with or against God's will. Russian literature frequently grapples with this freedom, portraying characters at crossroads, making decisions that align or conflict with moral law, thus illustrating the fundamental Catholic belief in the importance of free will in the economy of salvation.

The notion of universal salvation, while not universally accepted within Catholic doctrine, offers a hopeful outlook on the possibility of redemption for all souls, irrespective of their earthly sins. This perspective fosters a more inclusive view of salvation, resonating with the inclusive narrative strategies employed by Russian authors, who often present a diverse array of characters, each navigating their unique spiritual journey.

Furthermore, the Catholic Church's teachings on the efficacy of prayer and intercession for the souls in Purgatory highlight the communal aspect of salvation. Russian literature echoes this communal spirituality, demonstrating how characters' fates are interwoven, and hinting at a collective journey towards redemption.

In conclusion, the Catholic doctrines of personal judgment and universal salvation bring to light the complex interplay between divine justice and mercy. Russian literature, with its deep engagement with characters' moral and spiritual crises, serves as a rich field for exploring these theological themes. The narratives of Dostoyevsky and Tolstoy, in particular, offer profound insights into the nature of personal accountability and the boundless scope of divine forgiveness, reflecting a nuanced understanding of Catholic eschatological beliefs.

The wrestling with these concepts in literature not only enriches the understanding of Catholic theology but also invites readers into a deeper contemplation of their own beliefs regarding judgment, redemption, and the universality of God's salvific will. As such, the exploration of personal judgment and universal salvation in Russian literature not only highlights the impact of Catholic thought on these literary giants but also underscores the enduring relevance of these doctrines in navigating the existential queries that define the human condition.

The Eternal Dialogue - Catholicism's Living Legacy in Russian Literature

The exploration of Catholicism's imprint on Russian literature is not merely an academic endeavor but a voyage into the depths of the human spirit, as mirrored in the masterworks of Dostoyevsky and Tolstoy. This eternal dialogue between faith and literature illuminates the profound ways in which Catholic doctrine and spirituality have woven themselves into the fabric of Russian narrative art, challenging and nurturing its growth. While examining this legacy, it's crucial to acknowledge the fertile ground from which such a relationship could sprout and the fruit it bore, influencing both the literary landscape and the spiritual introspection of its devout readership.

The intertwining of Catholic theology with the storytelling prowess of Russia's literary giants has presented an unparalleled view into the complexities of free will, divine justice, and the search for God. Dostoyevsky's narrative vividly illustrates the Catholic understanding of suffering and redemption, positing that through suffering, one finds a path to redemption, echoing Christ's own passion and resurrection. Tolstoy's works, although often grappling with dogmatic religion, nonetheless engage deeply with the Catholic envisioning of the Kingdom of God within the individual, emphasizing the ethical imperatives of love and nonviolence.

Further, the narrative journey of sin, confession, forgiveness, and the eventual return to faith outlines a distinctly Catholic arc of redemption that is mirrored in Russian literature's great prodigal sons. This arc not only aligns with the sacramental life of the Church but also with its moral and spiritual teachings, inviting a continual return to God's mercy and love. The presence of Catholic sacraments and symbols—significantly the cross as a motif of suffering and salvation—within these narratives adds layers of meaning and aids in the deepening of their thematic richness.

In dialogues on faith, both implicit and explicit, Russian literature engages with philosophical disputation and inner monologues that reflect an intellectual struggle with atheism and the discernment of divine will. Such engagement is emblematic of the Catholic intellectual tradition's emphasis on the marriage of faith and reason, encouraging readers to embark on their own spiritual and intellectual journeys.

The veneration of the Virgin Mary, as both a symbol of the Church and a mother figure, brings forth the nurturing, compassionate face of Catholicism into Russian narratives. This Marian devotion aligns with Catholic teachings on Mary's intercessory power and her role as a mediator of divine compassion, further enriching the spiritual dimensions of these literary works.

Mystical experiences and encounters with the divine featured in Russian literature also speak to the influence of Catholic mysticism, inviting readers into a contemplation of the transcendent and the presence of God in everyday life. This mystical undercurrent challenges the boundaries between the divine and the mundane, urging a deeper, more intimate engagement with the divine mystery.

The moral landscape of Russian literature, with its emphasis on charity, works of mercy, personal conversion, and community, finds resonance with Catholic moral theology. These narratives hold up a mirror to the virtues and moral choices that define the human condition, engaging with the Catholic conception of living a life oriented towards love and service to others.

In depicting the Church as both militant and triumphant, battling evil while celebrating the communion of saints, Russian literature parallels Catholic eschatological themes. The concepts of afterlife, ultimate justice, personal judgment, and universal salvation become arenas for exploring the human soul's destiny and the cosmic struggle between good and evil.

As this book closes, it's essential to reflect upon the eternal dialogue between Catholicism and Russian literature not as a concluded conversation but as an ongoing discourse—a living legacy that continues to influence and inspire. This dialogue transcends temporal boundaries, inviting not only Roman Catholics, Russian Literature Scholars, Ethicists, Moral Theologians, and Students into its fold but also anyone who navigates the human experience through the lens of faith and literature.

The legacy of Catholicism in Russian literature serves as a testament to the enduring power of faith to shape and enrich the human story. Bearing witness to this legacy calls us to appreciate the beauty and depth of the dialogue that can exist between religion and art, faith and culture. It is a reminder of the potential for literature and spirituality to mutually enrich and transform one another, bringing to light the deeper truths of the human condition and the quest for meaning, purpose, and transcendence.

In conclusion, the living legacy of Catholicism in Russian literature is a vivid example of how deeply faith can inform art, shaping not only the narrative arcs of great literary works but also the hearts and minds of their readers. The eternal dialogue between Catholicism and Russian literature is a beacon of the ongoing conversation between the divine and the human, offering rich insights into the complexities of faith, the struggles of the human soul, and the redemptive power of grace.

Appendix A: Key Catholic Doctrines and Their Interpretation in Russian Literature

The nexus between Catholic doctrines and the labyrinthine world of Russian literature unveils a compelling discourse on spirituality, morality, and human existentialism. This appendix endeavors to delineate the intricacies of Catholic theology as they are woven into the fabric of Russian literary masterpieces, primarily focusing on the works of Dostoyevsky and Tolstoy, whose narratives are imbued with profound theological inquiries and moral contemplations.

In essence, the doctrine of free will, a cornerstone of Catholic teaching, finds a resonant echo in Russian literary discourse. The struggles and triumphs of Dostoyevsky's characters, notably in "The Brothers Karamazov," illuminate the Catholic understanding of human freedom juxtaposed with divine grace (Dostoyevsky, 1880). Here, the moral quagmires and spiritual awakenings of the characters encapsulate the Catholic dogma that while humans are graced with free will, their salvation ultimately hinges upon their openness to divine grace and mercy.

Suffering, as a path to redemption, is another cardinal Catholic doctrine mirrored in the annals of Russian fiction. This tenet posits that through suffering, one's soul is purified and brought closer to God. Tolstoy's "War and Peace" and Dostoyevsky's "Crime and Punishment" present a vivid panorama of characters whose encounters with suffering serve as a crucible for spiritual refinement and moral redemption (Tolstoy, 1869; Dostoyevsky, 1866).

The sacrament of confession, integral to Catholic doctrine, finds its literary counterpart in the theme of confession as a means of unburdening one's soul, evident in the soul-baring monologues of Dostoyevsky's protagonists. The act of confession, both as a sacrament and a literary motif, underscores the belief in the power of verbalizing one's innermost sins and struggles as a step towards redemption.

Moreover, the Catholic dogma of the communion of saints and the intercessory power of the Virgin Mary resonate within the Russian literary tradition through the recurring motif of characters seeking guidance and intercession from figures embodying purity and holiness. This mirrors the Catholic belief in the spiritual solidarity that binds the faithful on Earth with the saints in heaven.

The eternal struggle between good and evil, a theme ubiquitous in both Catholic doctrine and Russian literature, reveals the complexity of human nature and the omnipresent battle for the soul's salvation. In this context, characters in Russian novels often embody the Catholic teaching on the inherent tendency towards sin (concupiscence) and the necessity of divine grace for salvation.

Catholicism's eschatological doctrines, encompassing concepts of heaven, hell, and the final judgment, are intricately explored in Russian literature, particularly in the symbolic representations of finality and judgment. These narratives probe the depths of human conscience and the divine criteria of judgment, reflecting the Catholic conviction of an afterlife where souls are recompensed according to their earthly lives.

The sacramental vision of life, a fundamental aspect of Catholic theology, emphasizing the presence of the divine in the mundane, finds its literary echo in the sacramental imagery pervasive in Russian literature. This perspective fosters a recognition of the sacred in the ordinary, inviting readers to perceive the divine grace that suffuses everyday existence.

Marian devotion, a distinguished element of Catholic spirituality, is mirrored in the veneration of maternal figures in Russian literature, who often embody compassion, intercession, and moral guidance, reflecting the Catholic reverence for the Virgin Mary as the epitome of maternal virtue and sanctity.

The virtue of charity, pivotal in Catholic moral theology, underpins numerous narratives in Russian literature, highlighting the transformative power of acts of kindness and self-giving love. This confluence underscores the universal call to live out the Gospel's command to love one's neighbor, a principle that transcends the boundaries of literature and doctrine.

In summary, the interpretive exploration of key Catholic doctrines within the purview of Russian literature unveils a dialogical relationship between faith and art. This relationship not only enriches our understanding of these literary works but also offers a profound insight into the universality and transcendent nature of Catholic theological principles. As Russian literature reflects and critiques these doctrines, it also contributes to the ongoing dialogue between faith and culture, demonstrating the enduring influence of Catholicism in the realm of human creativity and intellectual inquiry.

Appendix B: A Comparative Analysis of the Original Russian Texts and Their Catholic Themes

The exploration of Catholicism's resonance within classic Russian literature necessitates a focused analysis of the original texts by Fyodor Dostoyevsky and Leo Tolstoy. This appendix delves into a comparative study, shedding light on how these authors intricately wove Catholic themes into the fabric of their narratives, enriching their textual universe with profound spiritual and theological dimensions.

The canon of Russian literature, particularly the works of Dostoyevsky and Tolstoy, serves as a fertile ground for discerning the influence of Catholic thought. Despite the prevailing Orthodox Christian milieu of their era, both writers exhibited a remarkable openness to Catholic ideas, which they integrated into their literary masterpieces in various nuanced ways. This integration was not merely incidental; rather, it was a deliberate attempt to grapple with the universal questions of human existence, morality, and divinity, transcending the boundaries of their own cultural and religious upbringing.

At the heart of Dostoyevsky's narrative universe lies a profound engagement with the question of free will— a central theme in Catholic theology. This theological concept is deftly explored in his emblematic work, "The Brothers Karamazov," where the internal struggles and moral dilemmas faced by the characters serve as a reflection on the human capacity for choice between good and evil. The portrayal of Ivan Karamazov's existential doubt juxtaposed with Alyosha's unwavering faith highlights the tension between divine justice and human morality, presenting a rich tapestry for theological reflection.

Tolstoy, on the other hand, invites readers into a meticulous exploration of the ethical imperatives of love and nonviolence in "War and Peace" and "Anna Karenina." His narrative manifests a deep resonance with the Catholic understanding of agape— unconditional, sacrificial love — as the foundation of Christian ethics. Tolstoy's characters often embark on profound inner journeys, wrestling with their conscience and societal norms, in search of a higher moral ground informed by Christian love and compassion.

The theme of suffering and redemption, particularly evident in Dostoyevsky's "Crime and Punishment," encapsulates the essence of the Catholic view on redemptive suffering. The protagonist, Raskolnikov, embodies the archetype of the sinner seeking salvation through acknowledgment of guilt and acceptance of suffering as a pathway to redemption. This narrative arc is emblematic of the Catholic sacrament of confession, where the act of contrition opens the door to spiritual renewal and divine forgiveness.

Intriguingly, both authors intricately weave the sacramentals and symbols of Catholicism into the fabric of their stories. For instance, the recurrent image of the cross in Dostoyevsky's works serves as a profound symbol of suffering, sacrifice, and ultimately, salvation — mirroring the Catholic appreciation of the cross as central to the Christian narrative of redemption.

The Virgin Mary emerges as a pivotal figure in the dialogues on faith that permeate Russian literature. Her maternal compassion and intercessory power resonate profoundly with characters facing moral crises, mirroring the Catholic veneration of Mary as a symbol of the Church and embodiment of divine mercy. Her presence in the narratives serves as a beacon of hope and a source of comfort to the troubled souls, guiding them towards a deeper encounter with the divine.

The contemplation of the afterlife and concepts of heaven and hell is another area where the influence of Catholic theology is palpable. Both Dostoyevsky and Tolstoy engage with eschatological themes, probing the mysteries of death, judgment, and the ultimate fate of the soul. These existential inquiries reflect Catholic teachings on the afterlife as the ultimate justice, offering a vision of hope and redemption beyond the temporal confines of earthly existence.

The presence of the mystical and transcendent in the works of both authors highlights the influence of Catholic mysticism, which emphasizes the experience of God's immediate presence and the soul's union with the divine. This mystical dimension opens new avenues for understanding the complex relationship between the divine and the human, inviting readers to transcend the empirical world and embrace the mystery of faith.

The intellectual struggle with atheism and the discernment of divine will are also pivotal themes that reveal the Catholic underpinnings of Russian literary discourse. Characters grappling with doubts about God's existence and seeking to understand the divine purpose in the midst of suffering and injustice embody the philosophical and theological debates that are central to Catholic thought.

In conclusion, the comparative analysis of the original Russian texts and their Catholic themes unearths the intricate ways in which Dostoyevsky and Tolstoy engaged with Catholic theology and philosophy. Through their literary genius, they opened a dialogue between faith and doubt, morality and redemption, weaving a profound narrative tapestry that continues to resonate with readers across cultures and epochs.

References

1. Givens, J. (2018). The Image of Christ in Russian Literature: Dostoevsky, Tolstoy, Bulgakov, Pasternak. Germany: Cornell University Press.

2. Harrison, E. A. (2013). The Development of the Image of Catholicism in Russian Literary Tradition, 1820-1949. (n.p.): University of London.

3. Balthasar, H. U., et al. (1990). Mary for Today. Ignatius Press.

4. Zendher, C. & Herlth, J. (Ed.). Models of Personal Conversion in Russian Cultural History of the 19th and 20th Centuries. (2015). Austria: Peter Lang.

5. Catechism of the Catholic Church. (1993). Libreria Editrice Vaticana.

6. Catechism of the Catholic Church. (1993). Vatican.va.

7. Catechism of the Catholic Church. (1994). 2nd ed. Vatican: Libreria Editrice Vaticana.

8. Catechism of the Catholic Church. (1994). Libreria Editrice Vaticana.

9. Catechism of the Catholic Church. (1994). Vatican City: Libreria Editrice Vaticana.

10. Dostoyevsky, F. (1866). Crime and Punishment.

11. Dostoyevsky, F. (2004). The Brothers Karamazov. Farrar, Straus and Giroux.

12. John Paul II. (1984). Reconciliatio et Paenitentia. Vatican: Libreria Editrice Vaticana.

13. John Paul II. (1984). Salvifici Doloris. Vatican City: Libreria Editrice Vaticana.

14. John Paul II. (1993). Veritatis Splendor. Vatican.va.

15. Green, M. (1986). The Origins of Nonviolence: Tolstoy and Gandhi in Their Historical Settings. United States: Pennsylvania State University Press.

16. Jones, M. V. (2005). Dostoyevsky and the Dynamics of Religious Experience. Anthem Press.

17. Pope Benedict XVI. (2007). Spe Salvi. Vatican.va.

18. Tolstoy, L. (2006). War and Peace. Vintage Classics.

19. Vatican Council II. (1964). Lumen Gentium. Vatican City: Libreria Editrice Vaticana.

20. Vatican II. (1965). Gaudium et Spes. Vatican.va.

21. Ramet, S. (ed.). Catholicism and Politics in Communist Societies. (1990). United Kingdom: Duke University Press.

22. Wojtyla, K. (1981). Love and Responsibility. Ignatius Press.

THE 15 PRAYERS OF ST. BRIDGET

 These Prayers and these Promises have been copied from a book printed in Toulouse in 1740 and published by the P. Adrien Parvilliers of the Company of Jesus, Apostolic Missionary of the Holy Land, with approbation, permission and recommendation to distribute them.
Pope Pius IX took cognisance of these Prayers with the prologue; he approved them May 31, 1862, recognising them as true and for the good of souls.

As St. Bridget for a long time wanted to know the number of blows Our Lord received during His Passion, He one day appeared to her and said: "I received 5480 blows on My Body. If you wish to honour them in some way, say 15 Our Fathers and 15 Hail Marys with the following Prayers (which He taught her) for a whole year. When the year is up, you will have honoured each one of My Wounds."

He made the following promises to anyone who recited these Prayers for a whole year:

1. I will deliver 15 souls of his lineage from Purgatory.

2. 15 souls of his lineage will be confirmed and preserved in grace.

3. 15 sinners of his lineage will be converted.

4. Whoever recites these Prayers will attain the first degree of perfection.

5. 15 days before his death I will give him My Precious Body in order that he may escape eternal starvation; I will give him My Precious Blood to drink lest he thirst eternally.

6. 15 days before his death he will feel a deep contrition for all his sins and will have a perfect knowledge of them.

7. I will place before him the sign of My Victorious Cross for his help and defence against the attacks of his enemies.

8. Before his death I shall come with My Dearest Beloved Mother.

9. I shall graciously receive his soul, and will lead it into eternal joys.

10. And having led it there I shall give him a special draught from the fountain of My Deity, something I will not for those who have not recited My Prayers.

11. Let it be known that whoever may have been living in a state of mortal sin for 30 years, but who will recite devoutly, or have the intention to recite these Prayers, the Lord will forgive him all his sins.

12. I shall protect him from strong temptations.

13. I shall preserve and guard his 5 senses.

14. I shall preserve him from a sudden death.

15. His soul will be delivered from eternal death.

16. He will obtain all he asks for from God and the Blessed Virgin.

17. If he has lived all his life doing his own will and he is to die the next day, his life will be prolonged.

18. Every time one recites these Prayers he gains 100 days indulgence.

19. He is assured of being joined to the supreme Choir of Angels.

20. Whoever teaches these Prayers to another, will have continuous joy and merit which will endure eternally.

21. There where these Prayers are being said or will be said in the future God is present with His grace.

Each prayer is preceded by one Our Father and one Hail Mary.

Our Father, who art in heaven, hallowed be thy name.
Thy kingdom come.
Thy will be done on earth as it is in heaven.
Give us this day our daily bread and forgive us our
trespasses as we forgive those who trespass against us and
lead us not into temptation but deliver us from evil. **Amen**

Hail Mary, full of grace, the Lord is with thee; blessed art
thou among women and blessed is the fruit of thy womb,
Jesus.
Holy Mary, Mother of God, pray for us sinners, now and at
the hour of our death. **Amen.**

FIRST PRAYER
Our Father – Hail Mary.
O Jesus Christ! Eternal Sweetness to those who love Thee,
joy surpassing all joy and all desire, Salvation and Hope of
all sinners, Who hast proved that Thou hast no greater
desire than to be among men, even assuming human nature
at the fullness of time for the love of men, recall all the
sufferings Thou hast endured from the instant of Thy
conception, and especially during Thy Passion, as it was

decreed and ordained from all eternity in the Divine plan.

Remember, O Lord, that during the Last Supper with Thy disciples, having washed their feet, Thou gavest them Thy Most Precious Body and Blood, and while at the same time thou didst sweetly console them, Thou didst foretell them Thy coming Passion.
Remember the sadness and bitterness which Thou didst experience in Thy Soul as Thou Thyself bore witness saying: "My Soul is sorrowful even unto death."

Remember all the fear, anguish and pain that Thou didst suffer in Thy delicate Body before the torment of the Crucifixion, when, after having prayed three times, bathed in a sweat of blood, Thou wast betrayed by Judas, Thy disciple, arrested by the people of a nation Thou hadst chosen and elevated, accused by false witnesses, unjustly judged by three judges during the flower of Thy youth and during the solemn Paschal season.

Remember that Thou wast despoiled of Thy garments and clothed in those of derision; that Thy Face and Eyes were veiled, that Thou wast buffeted, crowned with thorns, a reed placed in Thy Hands, that Thou was crushed with blows and overwhelmed with affronts and outrages.
In memory of all these pains and sufferings which Thou didst endure before Thy Passion on the Cross, grant me before my death true contrition, a sincere and entire confession, worthy satisfaction and the remission of all my sins. **Amen.**

SECOND PRAYER
Our Father – Hail Mary.
O Jesus! True liberty of angels, Paradise of delights, remember the horror and sadness which Thou didst endure when Thy enemies, like furious lions, surrounded Thee, and by thousands of insults, spits, blows, lacerations and other unheard-of-cruelties, tormented Thee at will.

In consideration of these torments and insulting words, I beseech Thee, O my Saviour, to deliver me from all my enemies, visible and invisible, and to bring me, under Thy protection, to the perfection of eternal salvation. **Amen.**

THIRD PRAYER
Our Father - Hail Mary.
O Jesus! Creator of Heaven and earth Whom nothing can encompass or limit, Thou Who dost enfold and hold all under Thy Loving power, remember the very bitter pain.

Thou didst suffer when the Jews nailed Thy Sacred Hands and Feet to the Cross by blow after blow with big blunt nails, and not finding Thee in a pitiable enough state to satisfy their rage, they enlarged Thy Wounds, and added pain to pain, and with indescribable cruelty stretched Thy Body on the Cross, pulled Thee from all sides, thus dislocating Thy Limbs.

I beg of Thee, O Jesus, by the memory of this most Loving suffering of the Cross, to grant me the grace to fear Thee and to Love Thee. **Amen.**

FOURTH PRAYER
Our Father - Hail Mary.
O Jesus! Heavenly Physician, raised aloft on the Cross to heal our wounds with Thine, remember the bruises which Thou didst suffer and the weakness of all Thy Members which were distended to such a degree that never was there pain like unto Thine.

From the crown of Thy Head to the Soles of Thy Feet there was not one spot on Thy Body that was not in torment, and yet, forgetting all Thy sufferings, Thou didst not cease to pray to Thy Heavenly Father for Thy enemies, saying:

"Father forgive them for they know not what they do."

Through this great Mercy, and in memory of this suffering, grant that the remembrance of Thy Most Bitter Passion may effect in us a perfect contrition and the remission of all our sins. **Amen**.

FIFTH PRAYER
Our Father - Hail Mary.
O Jesus! Mirror of eternal splendour, remember the sadness which Thou experienced, when contemplating in the light of Thy Divinity the predestination of those who would be saved by the merits of Thy Sacred Passion.

Thou didst see at the same time, the great multitude of reprobates who would be damned for their sins, and Thou didst complain bitterly of those hopeless lost and unfortunate sinners.

Through this abyss of compassion and pity, and especially through the goodness which Thou displayed to the good thief when Thou saidst to him: "This day, thou shalt be with Me in Paradise." I beg of Thee, O Sweet Jesus, that at the hour of my death, Thou wilt show me mercy. **Amen**.

SIXTH PRAYER
Our Father - Hail Mary.
O Jesus! Beloved and most desirable King, remember the grief Thou didst suffer, when naked and like a common criminal.

Thou was fastened and raised on the Cross, when all Thy relatives and friends abandoned Thee, except Thy Beloved Mother, who remained close to Thee during Thy agony and whom Thou didst entrust to Thy faithful disciple when Thou saidst to Mary: "Woman, behold thy son!" and to St. John:

"Son, behold thy Mother!"

I beg of Thee O my Saviour, by the sword of sorrow which pierced the soul of Thy holy Mother, to have compassion on me in all my affliction and tribulations, both corporal and spiritual, and to assist me in all my trials, and especially at the hour of my death. **Amen**.

SEVENTH PRAYER
Our Father – Hail Mary.
O Jesus! Inexhaustible Fountain of compassion, Who by a profound gesture of Love, said from the Cross: "I thirst!" suffered from the thirst for the salvation of the human race.

I beg of Thee O my Saviour, to inflame in our hearts the desire to tend toward perfection in all our acts; and to extinguish in us the concupiscence of the flesh and the ardor of worldly desires. **Amen**.

EIGHTH PRAYER
Our Father – Hail Mary.
O Jesus! Sweetness of hearts, delight of the spirit, by the bitterness of the vinegar and gall which Thou didst taste on the Cross for Love of us, grant us the grace to receive worthily.

Thy Precious Body and Blood during our life and at the hour of our death, that they may serve as a remedy and consolation for our souls. **Amen.**

NINTH PRAYER
Our Father – Hail Mary.
O Jesus! Royal virtue, joy of the mind, recall the pain Thou didst endure when, plunged in an ocean of bitterness at the approach of death, insulted, outraged by the Jews.

Thou didst cry out in a loud voice that Thou was abandoned by Thy Father, saying: "My God, My God, why hast Thou forsaken me?"

Through this anguish, I beg of Thee, O my Saviour, not to abandon me in the terrors and pains of my death. **Amen.**

TENTH PRAYER
Our Father - Hail Mary.
O Jesus! Who art the beginning and end of all things, life and virtue, remembers that for our sakes Thou was plunged in an abyss of suffering from the soles of Thy Feet to the crown of Thy Head.

In consideration of the enormity of Thy Wounds, teach me to keep, through pure love, Thy Commandments, whose way is wide and easy for those who love Thee. **Amen.**

ELEVENTH PRAYER
Our Father - Hail Mary.
O Jesus! Deep abyss of mercy, I beg of Thee, in memory of Thy Wounds which penetrated to the very marrow of Thy Bones and to the depth of Thy being, to draw me, a miserable sinner, overwhelmed by my offenses, away from sin and to hide me from Thy Face justly irritated against me, hide me in Thy wounds, until Thy anger and just indignation shall have passed away. **Amen.**

TWELFTH PRAYER
Our Father - Hail Mary.
O Jesus! Mirror of Truth, symbol of unity, bond of charity, remember the multitude of wounds with which Thou wast afflicted from head to foot, torn and reddened by the spilling of Thy adorable Blood. O great and universal pain, which

Thou didst suffer in Thy virginal flesh for love of us! Sweetest Jesus! What is there that Thou couldst have done for us which Thou has not done!

May the fruit of Thy suffering be renewed in my soul by the faithful remembrance of Thy Passion, and may Thy love increase in my heart each day, until I see Thee in eternity: Thou Who art the treasure of every real good and every joy, which I beg Thee to grant me, O Sweetest Jesus, in heaven. **Amen.**

THIRTEENTH PRAYER
Our Father - Hail Mary.
O Jesus! Strong Lion, Immortal and Invincible King, remember the pain which Thou didst endure when all Thy strength, both moral and physical, was entirely exhausted, Thou didst bow Thy Head, saying: "It is consummated!"

Through this anguish and grief, I beg of Thee Lord Jesus, to have mercy on me at the hour of my death when my mind will be greatly troubled and my soul will be in anguish. **Amen.**

FOURTEENTH PRAYER
Our Father - Hail Mary.
O Jesus! Only Son of the Father, Splendour and Figure of His Substance, remember the simple and humble recommendation.

Thou didst make of Thy Soul to Thy Eternal Father, saying: "Father, into Thy Hands I commend My Spirit!" And with Thy Body all torn, and Thy Heart Broken, and the bowels of Thy Mercy open to redeem us, Thou didst Expire.

By this Precious Death, I beg of Thee O King of Saints, comfort me and help me to resist the devil, the flesh and the world, so that being dead to the world I may live for Thee alone.

I beg of Thee at the hour of my death to receive me, a pilgrim and an exile returning to Thee. **Amen.**

FIFTEENTH PRAYER
Our Father - Hail Mary.
O Jesus! True and fruitful Vine! Remember the abundant outpouring of Blood which Thou didst so generously shed from Thy Sacred Body as juice from grapes in a wine press.

From Thy Side, pierced with a lance by a soldier, blood and water issued forth until there was not left in Thy Body a single drop, and finally, like a bundle of myrrh lifted to the top of the Cross Thy delicate Flesh was destroyed, the very Substance of Thy Body withered, and the Marrow of Thy Bones dried up.

Through this bitter Passion and through the outpouring of Thy Precious Blood, I beg of Thee, O Sweet Jesus, to receive my soul when I am in my death agony. **Amen.**

CONCLUSION
O Sweet Jesus! Pierce my heart so that my tears of penitence and love will be my bread day and night; may I be converted entirely to Thee, may my heart be Thy perpetual habitation, may my conversation be pleasing to Thee, and may the end of my life be so praiseworthy that I may merit Heaven and there with Thy saints, praise Thee forever. **Amen.**